Competency-based Recruitment and Selection

THE WILEY SERIES
in
STRATEGIC HUMAN RESOURCE MANAGEMENT

Series Editor

Neil Anderson
Goldsmiths College, University of London

Competency-based Recruitment and Selection
Robert Wood and Tim Payne

Further titles in preparation

Deception in Selection
Liz Walley and Mike Smith

Trust and Transition: Managing the Employment Relationship
Peter Herriot, Wendy Hirsh and Peter Reilly

Competency-based Recruitment and Selection

Robert Wood and Tim Payne

JOHN WILEY & SONS

Chichester • New York • Weinheim • Brisbane • Singapore • Toronto

Other Wiley Editorial Offices

John Wiley & Sons Inc., 111 River Street, Hoboken, NJ 07030, USA

Jossey-Bass, 989 Market Street, San Francisco, CA 94103-1741, USA

Wiley-VCH Verlag GmbH, Boschstr. 12, D-69469 Weinheim, Germany

John Wiley & Sons Australia Ltd, 33 Park Road, Milton, Queensland 4064, Australia

John Wiley & Sons (Asia) Pte Ltd, 2 Clementi Loop #02-01, Jin Xing Distripark, Singapore 129809

John Wiley & Sons (Canada) Ltd, 22 Worcester Road, Etobicoke, Ontario M9W 1L1

Wiley also publishes its books in a variety of electronic formats. Some content that appears in
print may not be available in electronic books.

Library of Congress Cataloguing in Publication Data
Wood, Robert.
    Competency-based recruitment and selection / Robert Wood and Tim Payne.
        p. cm. — (The Wiley series in strategic human resource management)
    Includes bibliographical references and index.
    ISBN 0-471-97473-0
    1. Employees–Recruiting. 2. Employee selection. I. Payne, Tim. II. Title. III.
Series.
    HF5549.5.R44W66   1998
    658.3´11—dc21   97–371044
                                                                                                                CIP

British Library Cataloguing in Publication Data
A catalogue record for this book is available from the British Library

ISBN 0-471-97473-0

Typeset in 10/12pt Palatino by York House Typographic Ltd, London
Printed and bound in Great Britain by Biddles Ltd, Guildford and King's Lynn.
This book is printed on acid-free paper responsibly manufactured from sustainable
forestry, for which at least two trees are planted for each one used.

Editorial Advisory Board

Contents

Series Editor's preface

Strategic Human Resource Management (HRM) has come of age. Fundamental and core changes in the nature of work and work organization have resulted in far reaching and universally felt changes in the practice of HRM in industry. Many departments which were formally known under the generic title of the 'personnel department', have reflected these inescapable changes by renaming the function the 'human resource management department'. But such changes in name alone do not reflect the more subtle, covert and pervasive themes of change which have afflicted the professional practice of HRM over the last decade or so. HRM has been transformed from being a welfare and administration oriented service department toward becoming a strategically-oriented and business policy-setting function which is responsible for much more than the hiring and firing of personnel.

Although the very term 'HRM' has provoked numerous charges of being one of mere empty rhetoric, few would doubt that the demands upon specialist human resource management departments have changed beyond all recognition over more recent years. Flexible forms of working, ad hoc project teams, decentralization, outsourcing of functions, and the devolvement of budgets are all factors which have contributed to the coming of age of the HR department. Yet we are far from witnessing the final, logical outcomes to such driving forces for change. Indeed, HR is a function and profession in transition. For this reason, it is important and timely for HR professionals, consultants, and practitioners to take stock of the current state of their profession and its concomitant methods, theories and procedures. For whilst the context within which HR is practised is changing rapidly, some would argue that the profession has struggled to keep pace with these drivers for change, and that simultaneously, whilst we have seen numerous attempts at innovative practice within HRM, there remains a stable backbone of traditional practice and practices in many industrial sectors.

The tensions within the HR profession have therefore become a paramount concern. Pressures towards cost-effectiveness and ultimatums to demonstrate the real world contribution of HR to any business enterprise do not sit easily alongside more academic treatises on what HR practitioners *should* be doing to stand at the forefront of innovative practice. In fact, some would argue that the practice of HR has become very much more market-driven over the last decade, and that the professional status of the HR body has taken second place behind the acute and day-to-day pressures faced by every practising HR manager in their own organizational setting. This second tension is between theory and practice and is one that has arguably led to an increasing divide between researchers and practitioners in HRM. If this has indeed been the case, this is an unfortunate outcome, as both sides of the profession can surely learn much from the other. Yet another tension concerns the professional responsibilities and reporting relationships of HR practitioners. Is the HR manager primarily a member of their own organization's management team, or a qualified professional bringing her or his own expertise to bear on this particular employing organization? Many practising HR managers will have felt this tension at some point in their careers, and the compelling pressures towards competitive advantage now both in the private and the public sectors of industry have resulted in HR professionals having to demonstrate the 'added value' of their work much more clearly than ever was the case in the past.

Given this changing context for the profession of HRM, the driving forces for business change, and the ambitions and career goals of practising HR managers, it is no surprise that those attempting to practise in the field in the late 1990s face a veritable barrage of conflicting pressures and role requirements. The HR manager has become everything to all employees: a member of the senior management team; a confidential friend and counsellor; an expert professional belonging to a recognized professional body; facilitator of organizational change; and manager of her or his own HRM department staff, to name but a few of the predominant roles. This lack of role clarity has led undoubtedly to feelings of stress and being a 'Jack of all trades' amongst many personnel professionals. So where might the way forward be? Although these conflicting pressures may well have led to role conflict, they have also opened up many doors of opportunity for practising at a strategic level within organizations. Organization development interventions, team building, stress management audits, senior managerial succession planning, employee reward systems, staff appraisal procedures, and contributing to the organization's vision and objectives are all areas which historically were absolute no-go zones for the 'people-people' in traditional personnel departments. Yet nowadays, HR professionals are *expected* to make a definite and tangible contribution to many of these areas. It is therefore timely to examine the practice of HR under the title of 'Strategic HRM'.

The objective of the Strategic HRM series is to bring together a collection of cutting-edge texts which examine and interpret some of the most pressing concerns for HRM practice in industry. All books in the series have been written by eminent and acknowledged experts in their own field of practice, whether they happen to be based in academia, consultancy, or industry. Indeed, the authors contributing to the series do originate from these three different backgrounds. The books attempt to bridge the academic– practitioner divide, but not in a bland matter-of-fact manner. Indeed, quite the opposite. Authors have been encouraged to be opinionated and to offer a personal commentary on what they believe as experts in their respective areas to be the predominant issues of concern for practising HR managers. Readers will therefore hopefully find all texts in the series thought provoking, carefully considered, but reasoned position statements on the current state-of-the-art of each area addressed by each book within the series. Books have been written to be easily accessible to the reader, but nevertheless, to challenge taken for granted assumptions and traditional practices in HRM. It is my hope, as Series Editor, that every reader will gain something from each book within the series, that readers will find as much to agree with as to disagree with in each text, but crucially, that all books provide a thought provoking account of changes within the HR profession. Although these house-style guidelines have been worked to by all authors contributing to this series, each volume will nevertheless show an individual style and format which is best suited to the material covered. A stringent and imposed editorial policy was therefore intentionally avoided, and indeed, the autonomy to present personal viewpoints, opinions, and suggestions for improvement in Strategic HRM was encouraged at all stages in the authoring and production process. Books cover a wide range of topics within Strategic HRM, and therefore are not intended as 'best practice' how-to texts. Given this diversity of subject matter and approach, it is my hope that the authors have indeed produced texts which will be of interest and concern to practising HR managers. In my view the authors have without exception done a diligent and splendid job in this respect and by so doing have contributed to the debate which promises to shape the future of strategic human resource management in this country.

Neil Anderson
Professor of Work Psychology

Acknowledgements

We would like to acknowledge our colleagues, past and present, who have helped to shape the contents of this book; also our clients, who have done likewise. We would particularly like to thank Yasmin Ahmed for her support and suggestions throughout, and Nicole Banerji and Chris Mulrooney for their helpful comments on earlier drafts of the book. Stevie Heath did a sterling job tracking down references and getting permissions. When it came to preparing the manuscript for publication, Sandra Macleod was brilliant – as usual.

Introduction

This is a 'how to' book based on our experience of implementing professional practice recruitment and selection processes. We deal with the whole cycle of recruitment and selection, from advertising, through shortlisting and assessing, to final decision making. Running through everything is the notion of *competencies*. Love it or loathe it, all we would say is that if it had not already been invented (and it has been, several times), it would be necessary to invent it. That is why competencies are not just any old flavour of the month. It was not always so, but so many HR policies and practices now depend crucially on having a structure around which everything can be integrated and harmonized. Inasmuch as competencies are serving that function, they cannot be blown away overnight. That is why we are sufficiently relaxed to believe a second edition of this book might be required in three or four years' time; providing this one is well received, naturally.

Using a running case study (a fictitious organization), and real examples from our own experience to illustrate specific points, we aim to guide the practitioner through the recruitment and selection maze. Although we are targeting external bulk selection, we will also try to make relevant connections for smaller organizations.

Both of us have experience of recruitment and selection methods from several perspectives. Between us, we have conducted academic and applied research into the effectiveness of different methods; we have designed and evaluated competency-based methods of recruitment and selection; we have used such methods to recruit and select professional staff into our own organization, and we have helped people in organizations to implement successfully a variety of competency-based procedures.

Drawing on our different personal experiences, we hope to be able to combine in this book the best practice aspects of recruitment and selection gleaned from academic and professional research, with the practical considerations important when implementing processes, as well as the leading edge methods developed in the field and not reported anywhere.

While each chapter is written so that it will 'stand alone', allowing you to dip in and out as you wish, there is also a natural ordering of chapters which corresponds to the ordering of events in a phased recruitment and selection process.

OVERVIEW OF THE BOOK

The book effectively falls into four sections:

- the context of recruitment and selection
- attracting and sifting candidates
- assessing candidates
- decision making and evaluating.

The context of recruitment and selection

Chapter 1 sets the scene. It introduces some of the key influences on recruitment and selection practices that are currently important. We also stick our necks out and predict how recruitment and selection are likely to go over the next few years.

In Chapter 2 we look at the key criteria on which practitioners base all recruitment and selection decisions. This brings us to competencies. We review the concept critically, bringing out assumptions, limitations and implications before going on to discuss how competencies can be used practically. In passing we mention the notion of 'competences' as utilized in British vocational qualifications. Since the meaning and application are quite different to what we are concerned with here, that is the only mention it gets.

In Chapter 3 we begin to look at the total selection process. We illustrate what the process might look like overall, from start to finish, and identify the key decisions which must be made up-front. We introduce the idea of utility, show how different combinations of assessment methods may be more or less appropriate depending on factors such as numbers of applicants, costs, predictive power of the methods, etc. We also consider issues of planning and resource availability which will determine the specifics of the system.

Attracting and sifting candidates

Chapter 4 is concerned with attracting candidates. We ask the question 'What are applicants looking for from an organization?', and present some data from our own research. We examine the factors which affect who applies to which organization, and how to present the most appropriate message when advertising. We spend some time looking at issues of fairness, particularly with respect to the benefits of diversity in the workforce, and how the recruitment and selection process can influence this. We also look at self-selection and how to appropriately trim response rates to a manageable size.

Chapter 5 is where we consider application form design and sifting. We discuss how competency-based application forms can work, how long they take to 'score', and how useful they are. We also examine alternatives to competency-based application forms, biodata and CVs. With recruiters and applicants now starting to utilize the Internet, we have something to say about the possibilities of this medium.

Assessing candidates

In Chapters 6 and 7 we deal with the most common method used for selection – the interview. This method remains so ubiquitous that it demands two chapters to itself. In Chapter 6 we discuss competency-based (structured) interviews, and other types of structured interviews; and in Chapter 7 we talk about how to use them in practice.

In Chapter 8 we discuss what is always a controversial topic – psychometrics. We deal with ability tests and personality questionnaires and examine how to pick and mix tests and questionnaires to suit a particular competency framework, and how to integrate information from psychometrics into the overall process.

Chapter 9 is where we talk about the assessment centre. This is perhaps the assessment method most closely associated with competencies, which is not surprising because competencies (or something like them) are needed to hold the whole thing together. We review the components of assessment centres, how to match competencies to exercises and what steps to go through when putting one together.

Decision making and evaluating

In Chapter 10 we examine how to make the overall selection decision. We look at ways of integrating the information collected about candidates; how much feedback to give, and to whom. We conclude with a discussion of what is involved in monitoring and evaluating the process.

THE CASE STUDY

To reinforce and dramatize what we are saying, we are going to run a case study throughout the book. The company in question is Fettercorn plc, a leading importer and distributor of exotic foodstuffs. Perhaps you have come across their Treenut Express and Mangomania ranges. You will meet Lupita Gonzalez, the MD, and Ros Fairburn, the Human Resource Manager, as well as some of their colleagues, and Jack, an independent occupational psychologist. They are going to be using competencies to recruit people and we will see how they get on. In particular, we will eavesdrop on how they propose to handle the recruitment and selection of a Head Buyer.

The context for recruitment and selection 1

Our purpose in this chapter is to set out the context for recruitment and selection now and into the next century (not such a grand claim; three years at the time of writing). To do this, we review seven current trends in the world of work, and make five predictions as to what may be important in the near future.

The aim of this book is to provide a practical guide to some of the issues that arise when implementing competency-based recruitment and selection processes (see Box 1.1 for our distinction between recruitment and selection). Practicality is important to us, and for that reason we would like to examine the subject within a realistic context – what are the real-life pressures on the people who have to make such systems work?

The context in which we must 'do' selection and recruitment is changing and changing fast. The assessment techniques, methods and approaches we use remain, for most organizations, unchanged. At the same time, enormous and rapid change in the way employers organize themselves is occurring. We need to be aware of these changes if our recruitment and selection methods are to work to their full potential. In the light of this, we have identified *seven* themes which seem to us likely to affect the way we go about recruitment and selection. We then go on to make *five* specific predictions about the ways recruitment and selection are likely to change in the next few years.

SEVEN THEMES IMPACTING ON RECRUITMENT AND SELECTION

The themes are:

1. Organizational changes.
2. Job changes.
3. Personal changes.

4. Societal changes.

5. Legislative changes.

6. Technological changes.

7. Marketing changes.

BOX 1.1   RECRUITMENT VERSUS SELECTION

Selection and recruitment are used interchangeably but we like to draw a distinction between the two. In our view, *recruitment* is a broad term used to communicate the notion of getting someone into the organization. As such, it covers everything from advertising to induction. Thus we talk about recruitment drives. But we would not talk about *selection* drives. Selection, for us, is focused at the point where a decision is made about who to recruit. As such, it is more concerned with the instruments and methods used to assess candidates.

---

1   Organizational changes

There is no doubt that organizations today are very different places to what they were 20 years ago. Whilst many of the changes that have and are taking place within industries have been well documented, it is rare that experts in the recruitment and selection business pause to think what such changes mean for them – how will the changes affect the way recruitment and selection are carried out?

Let us start with something dramatic – or melodramatic. Peter Drucker[1] has predicted that, to be competitive in future, organizations will need to achieve three times the productivity with only one third the number of people. That means fewer people, paid more, and doing more (anyone recognize this?).

To go to the particular, there is pressure from organizations able to operate globally in order to exploit the advantages of economies of scale and access to cheap labour. Bangalore in India is now a world centre for software programming. Your insurance claims are as likely to be processed now in Calcutta as in Coventry or Cleveland. There is pressure from the banks who, at least in the UK, are reluctant to sanction long-term loans and to work in partnership with organizations. This leads organizations to have to fund growth from efficiency savings within, which in turn squeezes the money available for R&D[2]. There is also pressure from the pension fund managers who now expect relatively huge dividend pay-ments each year, causing an emphasis on short-term profit and loss statements. The upshot of all this is that organizations are under pressure to:

- identify their core business, outsourcing whatever is left
- organize themselves around key processes rather than departments
- delayer, flatten and downsize (or 'rightsize', as the charming American euphemism has it).

But it is possible to go too far. The chief executive of British Gas, Richard Giordano, admitted (in February 1997) that in the latest reorganization there had been too much downsizing – by about 10,000 jobs. Little comfort there for those who were not so rightsized. The constant pressures to cut costs, be more creative and to do more with less resources certainly has improved efficiency, but there is a feeling that some organizations have lost valuable experience and expertise, and that the people remaining (the 'layoff survivors') are overstretched.

2   Job changes

As organizations have restructured, the structure of work – the nature of the job – has also changed. In his book *Job Shift*, William Bridges[3] has detailed the demise of the traditional, well defined job (at managerial level at least), with its clear tasks and clear accountabilities. In line with the move to customer-focused process working is a move towards cross-functional teams, roles aligned to the process rather than to the function, and the emphasis on supplying your own value-added contribution.

Perhaps jobs as such were never going to be particularly appropriate for the modern organization. Lawler, for example, has long argued[4] for organizations to be based around competencies rather than jobs. Then there is the concept of 'work parcels', which colleagues at Pearn Kandola are looking at. The idea is that, by matching the individual's knowledge, skills and attitudes to the required tasks and the contexts in which they are to be done, people end up doing 'parcels' of work for which they are best suited.

3   Personal changes

The changes in the nature of work have been reflected in a change in the nature of the contract of work. This is both a material change, for example the rise of fixed-term contracts, and a psychological change. The nature of the new psychological contract has been well described by Peter Herriot and Carol Pemberton[5]. Twenty years ago, they say, anyone who worked in a bank or insurance company knew that the psychological contract was loyalty in exchange for security; now that contract has been withdrawn. Table 1.1 shows how, in their view, the psychological contract has changed over the years.

Year	You offered (or offer)	Organization offered (or offers)
1975	• loyalty – not leaving • conformity – doing what you were asked • commitment – going the extra mile • trust – they'll keep their promises	• security of employment (job for life?) • promotion prospects • training • care when in trouble
1995	• long hours • added responsibility • broader skills • tolerance of change and ambiguity	• high pay • rewards for performance • a job

Table 1.1   Old and New Contracts[6]

As Herriot and Pemberton see it, not only has the 'new deal' been imposed but it is less than equitable to one of the sides – employees. That being so, what both parties to recruitment and selection will be looking for is bound to be affected. Employers will be looking more for people who can 'hit the ground running' and produce more or less instant returns; employees will be looking for employers who will develop and reward their skills.

4   Societal changes

Here we refer to the changing structure of society. That includes the increasing proportion of women workers and dual income families, also the growing proportions of ethnic minority workers, including citizens of other EU countries. Yet many of the assessment methods we use routinely have been designed by and trialled on white people for use in predominantly white organizations where fluency in the English language is automatically assumed. That world has changed for ever. Yes, there are still bastions of white middle-class maledom, but organizations are more and more coming to realize the potential benefits that a diverse workforce can bring.

Women's participation, in particular, will continue to increase. Looking at the percentage of women in full-time employment in the developed countries, in 1985 Spain stood lowest with 21 per cent; for figures reported in 1994 it was still lowest, but at 35.2 per cent. Sweden was the highest in 1985 with 82 per cent; in 1994 it stood at 90 per cent[7].

Like the United States, the UK has become a pluralist society, and employers are having to adapt, whether they like it or not. The number of students from what are presently called the ethnic minorities (but may not be for very much longer as assimilation accelerates) is growing. If organizations want the best, they are going to have to accept that this will inevitably lead to the recruitment of people with different backgrounds, values, attitudes and beliefs to those which are currently prevailing. They will also have to examine their selection methods to ensure that they are not excluding candidates because of extraneous factors (such as gender or age) rather than talent, ability or, as we might say, competence[8].

5   Legislative changes

In the UK we have for many years had legislation to deter unfair discrimination at the point of selection in terms of race and gender. The record on deterrence has been mixed but it would certainly have been worse had the legislation not been there. Now we have the Disability Discrimination Act which may prove to have the biggest impact of all. This is because, unlike race and gender, the Act absolutely places an obligation on recruiters and selectors to respond to whatever disabilities applicants present. To give a flavour of this, how do you manage the dyslexic applicant who is faced with a case study or in-tray exercise with a high written content? Or the partially sighted person who says they can tackle the test with a magnifying aid but has no idea (and you have no idea) how much extra time they might need? This is an area which has barely been scratched[9].

The next big issue could be age. Some publications are already refusing to take recruitment adverts which specify age limits. How can employers justify statements like 'the successful candidate will probably be under the age of 35'?

For organizations working across Europe, there are different emphases in the legislation in different member states. There are also different traditions and approaches to recruitment and selection, and different ways in which education and employment systems are geared in different countries (e.g. the French Grand Ecoles and the German 'meister' route). Superimposed on this are the recruitment practices of the truly European and global organizations which recruit not on a country-by-country basis, but on a world-wide basis. The implications of global recruitment remain to be explored.

6 Technological changes

Conventional methods of assessing competence are out of joint with the technology commonly in use in the workplace. Take in-tray exercises: how many people still have to deal with a paper-based in-tray? (Don't answer that. We know that it is more than we would like to think.) The fact is that for many people now, especially the young, it is second nature to communicate electronically. Yet how often on assessment centres (and we hold up our hands on this) do we expect candidates to illustrate their presentations with low tech aids like flip charts and hand-written acetates when packages such as Powerpoint are freely available? And how many organizations travel to university campuses to hand out paper-and-pencil tests when they could be asking applicants to complete tailored tests over the Internet?

It is obvious that electronic realizations of assessment devices can deliver results which are outside the scope of paper-and-pencil instruments[10]. This is more true of tests than questionnaires, which are always going to be just words on a page. It is the difference between dynamic and static representation of material. For example, a mechanical comprehension test item can be enhanced by depicting a clear and simple motion on the screen to help the test-taker better understand the particular properties of the motion in question. Many other examples could be given. Indeed, it will be a major disappointment, and the great loss of an opportunity, if test publishers restrict themselves to parallel versions and do not exploit the medium.

There are other advantages, too, which computers have over paper-and-pencil methods. There is adaptive testing, the possibility of varying the items you administer to an individual according to what the provisional estimate of that individual's ability is at any one time; the higher the estimate, the tougher the next item.

The acceptability of computerized testing is important – how do people respond? The general conclusion seems to be that people will respond favourably to computer-based tests, and that they will provide more or as much personal information as in a paper-and-pencil test or questionnaire. One study found that applicants reported greater test motivation with a computerized ability test than with the paper-and-pencil equivalent[11].

7 Marketing changes

There is a recruitment industry, and we would accept that we are a part of it. It includes the consultants, the test publishers, the IT systems developers, the recruitment agencies, and the headhunters. Like all industries, it has vested interests and flavours of the month. Competencies are a case in point – they are so much the paradigm of the moment that they have almost become a panacea for anything that ails ye on the human resources front ('You know what you need? A competency framework! ... ' 'I must have a competency framework – I'm not sure what I'll use it for, but I'll get one anyhow'.)

The marketing hype which surrounds the various products on the market today is a minefield which HR professionals will need to pick through warily. The claims made for products are less careful than they used to be. Take test publishers. Here is some publicity material one test publisher put out: 'helps you make the right management recruitment decisions – with total confidence'. Like most jingles, this is both jaunty and meaningless: 'help', which is partial, jars with 'total', which is complete. It could easily be a jingle for, say, a deodorant: 'helps you through those stress points in the day – with total confidence'. Or here is another publisher on its new range of ability tests, claimed quite unequivocally to be the *most significant improvement* in ability testing for 60 years. At least Carlsberg had the decency to say 'probably' the best lager in the world. This is what some of the launch blurb had to say: 'Would you like to transform your ability testing to achieve higher validities, *and* less bias against ethnic minorities? Come to our free seminar to find out how'. Users should not let this kind of hype go unchallenged; as ever, 'buyer beware' is the maxim.

FIVE PREDICTIONS FOR THE FUTURE OF RECRUITMENT AND SELECTION

As promised, we offer five sets of predictions for the future of recruitment and selection based on the trends outlined above. We also itemize the skills which will be required of professionals working in this area if our predictions come anywhere near true.*

1. The recruitment process will change.

2. Selection methods will change.

---

* This section is based on a report written for TSB. We thank them for their permission to re-use this material, which has however been heavily modified from the original.

3. What is being measured will change.

4. The focus of assessment will change.

5. Fairness and diversity issues will increasingly be on the agenda.

1. The recruitment process will change

There will be a shift in emphasis away from 'just' the selection instruments and selection events to include the attraction stage and the induction/ socialization stage.

Attraction

Attraction is going to become more and more important, particularly in graduate recruitment. The number of graduates coming out of universities is increasing faster than the number of graduate entry-level jobs. This will inevitably lead to higher numbers of applications, larger and less appropriate applicant pools, and increasing problems in managing and sifting these applicant pools. This will be particularly relevant to those organizations which have a high public profile. Organizations like these, we found from our own research[12], are more likely to attract speculative and untargeted applications from undergraduates. There will of course still be 'hot spots' where top graduates with specific skills can enjoy a seller's market. In such instances, we need to change the traditional approach to practices centred on the individual (how can we get those we want to accept our offers?). We look at attraction in detail in Chapter 4.

Induction

Induction is something more observed in the breach than in practice. It is quite possible that a poor induction process could cancel out all the effects of using a valid selection system (N. Anderson, personal communication). Conventional thinking about selection has stressed the importance of predicting job-specific fit. That, however, is only part of the story. Missing has been the appreciation that selection can also assist in the socialization of the individual towards the necessary person-organization fit without which that person cannot be fully effective. Where fit is achieved, employees can be expected to exhibit higher levels of satisfaction, commitment and performance, and lower levels of turnover, stress, and absenteeism. How applicants are handled when they begin their new jobs must receive increasing attention[13].

Skill requirement

Managing the recruitment image of your organization; managing large applicant pools, sifting these pools fairly and accurately; inducting new entrants with a special emphasis on the ongoing socialization of individuals into the organization.

---

2.   Selection methods will change

Over-exposure to published ability tests

This issue arises particularly in connection with graduate selection, where test familiarity is already an issue on the milk round, but it also impacts on the generation of managers selected with these tests over the last ten years. There are few widely available competitors to the SHL series, GMA series, Ravens Matrices and the Watson-Glaser. On the face of it, the new ABLE series offers a novel alternative to the market leaders, 'novel' because the tests attempt to simulate work situations, even if, at the time of writing, we have yet to see any validity evidence.

In the search for competitive advantage some organizations have turned towards custom-designed tests (Chase Manhattan, Fire Service) or work samples (British Airways, Inland Revenue, Employment Service). The absence of a licensing agreement and consequent savings usually compensate for the upfront development costs, particularly if the tests are to be used widely within the organization. Expect to see non-competing organizations banding together to commission tests for their exclusive use.

The relationship between test publisher and users

There is an issue around the regulation of test publishers, and their compliance to technical standards. It is all very well test publishers, or their representatives arguing that it is pointless getting worked up over technical quality issues when users have no interest in such matters. They may very well believe, if they think about it at all, that validity and reliability have already been taken care of before the product hits the market, but what if they are wrong, and it has not happened, or not happened enough? George Sik, who has associated himself with this view, likes to draw comparisons with cars[14]. When you buy a car, you assume it is safe. Tests, by extension, must be the same. But consider this. If a fault is discovered once a car is on the road, the manufacturer immediately seeks to withdraw the model. Given that cars are tested infinitely more rigorously than tests, our question would be, when has a test publisher ever withdrawn a product?

Test publishers cannot at the same time say that validity and reliability do not matter because the 'punter' does not care about them, yet continue to protect their products by requiring licensing fees, insisting that users attend training courses, charging for dongles (those things you stick on the back of PCs), and so forth. To do that, you have to have something validated to protect. That means being subject to regulation and to compliance disciplines, just as drug companies have to do before they can protect their patents. Without compliance disciplines the whole testing industry might as well be deregulated, and leave it to the free market to decide what happens. We can see this happening in any case, whether it is through tests becoming available on the Internet or, as Saville & Holdsworth did on Monday, January 13, 1997, by distributing, through *The Times*, a free version of one of their products. The first author, just the previous Wednesday (at the annual British Psychological Society Occupational Psychology Conference), had been making the point that if publishers could not substantiate the technical quality of their tests, then the tests might as well be sold in newsagents alongside puzzle magazines[15]. Little did he expect it to happen so soon. We consider issues around testing in Chapter 8.

Skill requirement

Knowledge of alternative published products and ability to evaluate the claims made in manuals (do not be one of those 'as long as it gets me from A to B' users); ability to judge when in-house tests should be commissioned; ability to manage consultants in their development and interpretation of the bespoke test specification.

Personality questionnaires

Everything that has just been said applies even with interest to personality questionnaires. We are being kind when we say there are products on the market which are 'cheap and cheerful'. Some might say 'quick and dirty'. At any rate, they are of dubious provenance. Personality questionnaires are perhaps the tools most open to abuse when used inappropriately, and it will be increasingly important to use them correctly. More generally, we see the distinction between personality measurement and other forms of performance rating disappearing fast. In a few years time we might wonder why we ever set out to measure 'personality' as a separate endeavour.

Whatever happens, keep a beady eye on computer-based personality questionnaires and expert system reports. These are gaining favour with personnel professionals, if not occupational psychologists. Their seemingly authoritative character is liable to lull people into thinking that they are more valid and reliable than they really are. Note that there is nothing to stop these computer-driven narrative reports being compiled by software writers who are not psychologists. Personality questionnaires are considered more fully in Chapter 8.

Skill requirement

Capacity to judge the quality of a personality questionnaire; to use them correctly and in the appropriate circumstances; knowledge of expert systems and their plus points and pitfalls.

Interviews

These are destined to remain the most popular selection/assessment method. After at least a decade of interview-bashing, academics are now coming round to supporting the structured interview in some of its forms. The validity of the interview when it is a structured interview done properly is better than it has ever been but that does not mean that worries about fairness have gone away. Technically, a major issue concerns the construct validity of interviews (to what extent do they measure social skills, motivation, communication skills, etc?). At present, all we know is that they measure multiple factors that predict job and training success. Another issue concerns how much interviews can contribute incrementally over ability tests, or vice-versa. We look at the principles of interviewing in Chapter 6, and deal with practical matters in Chapter 7.

Skill requirement

How to put together and use a structured interview; how to integrate the interview data with other data; how much weight to put on the interview.

Assessment centres

Assessment centres will increase in popularity, and their use will continue to expand from graduates and managers, both down to supervisors and shop-floor workers, and also upwards towards top managers and partners in professional firms. Their purpose will probably continue to be a mix of assessment and development, although we have seen an increase in the use of 'pure' development centres where the entire emphasis is on participants arriving at personal insights (NHSME, Oxford Regional Health Authority, Glaxo Wellcome, Chase Manhattan Bank). Three issues we would flag up are:

Standards

Expect a drive towards accreditation of assessors. It is inconsistent, is it not, to license people to administer and interpret test and questionnaire scores, but not to license assessors, whose performance may be altogether more determining of life chances than the odd test or questionnaire? But then, this may be just another instance of one of Murphy's laws – we license what is easiest to license.

Purpose

Perhaps because they are confused themselves, some organizations fail to tell staff whether centres are for assessment or development purposes, and some leave it deliberately ambiguous (it comes to the same thing), which does nothing for morale. If it is a development centre, the crucial thing is feedback, and the crucial action is doing it quickly, but not hastily. Here is an area where there is much lip service, but not a lot of action. How often is the feedback session put off, and off, especially if the manager giving the feedback was not actually present at the centre?

Fairness

There is a general perception that assessment centres are fair. This may be because on the surface they look more job related, or because they are intensive in terms of time and resource, or because they depend, as they do, on multiple sources of evidence. When assessment centres are designed properly and run by the book, in our experience they usually are fair. However we have come across centres where corners have been cut.

The complexity of assessment centres means that there is more opportunity for things to go wrong. For example, what was the makeup of the sample used for the job analysis? Do the exercises really measure the competencies or dimensions? Can this be demonstrated? Fairness in assessment centre use will become an issue. We delve into these issues further in Chapter 9.

Skill requirement

Be clear on your policy of assessment versus development centres, and make sure you can explain to participants exactly who will have what data and why; constantly evaluate your processes for designing, running and monitoring your centres in terms of fairness and best practice.

360° assessment

The use of competency-based self, peer, manager, even customer assessment questionnaires for development purposes is destined to grow and grow, even if the validity and reliability evidence which would support their use is conspicuous by its absence.

3.   What is being assessed will change

At the moment, competencies are king. This may not last, some would say will not last, although our position is that there will always be a need to summarize behaviour helpfully via an explanatory concept like 'ability' or 'trait'; at any rate, that has been true in psychological measurement for the past 60 years. But flavours of the month are, by definition, ephemeral, so be prepared for 'the next big thing'. Our guess is that it could be around the kind of individual attributes that are singled out for assessment. Perhaps, and we would be keen on this, there will be a greater emphasis on the more *psychological* aspects of an individual, for example:

Integrity and professional deviance

It is common for integrity, or honesty, to be tested in the United States. Quite reasonably, employers want to know how likely an employee is to be dishonest at work. This can range from the petty white collar embezzler (stamps and paper clips) to the major league swindlers (rogue traders and the like). The issue seems particularly relevant to financial institutions. To date, as far as we can tell, what are called integrity tests in the USA have not been much used in the UK, and may never be. The Boots Company did use one for a time with warehouse employees, but stopped when there were complaints about lack of trust. Another UK high street trader did some trialling but did not like what they saw, and pulled out. The distributors of the tests claimed, charmingly, that the tests could be used as a threat in the first instance, saying essentially that if you tell candidates at the recruitment stage that they will have to sit such a test you will soon put off the undesirables.

Baldry and Fletcher, authors of a recent review paper[16], made it clear that the decision to reject a candidate because they pose a high risk of engaging in deviant/dishonest behaviour is a conclusion that should be arrived at on the basis of more than just a score on one integrity test. This, of course, helps to make the point that when something is obviously at stake the validity and reliability of psychometric measures do indeed matter. More generally, Baldry and Fletcher argue that achieving high levels of integrity in an organization is not only (perhaps not even primarily) a selection problem. Organizations that practise as well as promote integrity and the wider aspects of 'organizational citizenship' need not concern themselves with integrity tests.

Learning ability

Management gurus tell us that the only constant left is that things will change. The implication of this is that workers will constantly have to learn and re-learn skills and knowledge. If that is right, and we think it is, then an important selection criterion must be 'How good at learning is this person?', which in turn raises development questions like 'How can we help people improve their learning skills?' or their 'flexibility' or 'adaptability'?

Mental health

Now that damages are being sought from organizations for causing stress-related illness, stress and stress tolerance (or 'resilience') may become an issue for assessment. Although most psychologists would argue that stress is a result of the interaction of the person and the environment, and that organizations should manage stress rather than select it out, 'resilience' is cropping up more and more as a competency.

Innovation and creativity

Although a bit of an old chestnut, the current pressures on organizations demand more and more creative solutions (i.e. how to do things better, cheaper, faster). Selecting for innovation and creativity is again going to become an issue.

Skill requirement

Become aware of integrity tests, the issues around their use and potential applications; identify/construct methods for assessing learning ability; identify the organizational position on stress with respect to assessment; explore what creativity means to your organization and find a way to tap into it.

---

4. The focus of assessment will change

High ability

High flyers will become even more of an issue. Is it worth identifying and fast-tracking high-flyers? Can you afford not to (even if you do not do it very well)? If so, how are they to be managed, developed and retained, or discarded? The tests on the market do not discriminate well between the good and the excellent performers. This is another area where custom-built tests may be required. Always remember, though, and this is a diversity argument, that talent can be found anywhere in the organization, not just among high flyers. Everyone will have their own story. One article tells of a sales assistant in Northern Electric (Retail) who sells, on average, £240 of electrical goods per hour; in comparison, bottom performers sell, on average, just £70 an hour[17].

Selection for redundancy

With the increase in rationalization and downsizing, selection for redundancy or for remaining jobs is becoming widespread. This issue is really a hot potato. Not surprisingly, employers are keeping quiet about what they are doing in this area, although occasionally we catch a glimpse of what may be the tip of a very large iceberg, e.g. Anglia Water, who may or may not have used personality profiles as part of their labour shedding process.

5.   Fairness and diversity issues will increasingly be on the agenda

Fairness issues have always been important when thinking about selection and assessment, and the scope of 'fairness' can only widen.

Litigation

Our society has become more litigious, and this is reflected in the increasing number of tribunals brought concerning unfair treatment during assessment. If your processes are unfair, it is likely that you will be taken to tribunal by someone sooner or later.

Quality of job analysis

In the USA, the courts have been much tougher in terms of their treatment of assessment cases. Often cases have turned on the quality of job analysis and job analysis methods.

Diversity and teams

There is mixed evidence that diverse teams are more effective than homogenous ones[18][19]. Selection techniques like biodata and unstructured interviews can have the effect of 'cloning', i.e. selecting people like the ones already employed, which will tend to decrease diversity.

Disability

Testing people with disabilities is an area much neglected, but it will need to be attended to, as a matter of urgency, because the Disability Discrimination Act puts the onus on employers to respond to whatever disabilities applicants for jobs present.

Age

Although not yet covered by law, there is increasing anger at the overt discrimination practised by many recruiters who put arbitrary age limits in adverts. This short-sighted practice may well be outlawed in the next few years.

Europe and globalization

As managers become more mobile across countries, assessment will need to be able to take into account different cultures and languages. At Pearn Kandola we have been asked to assess 'cultural adaptability' amongst managers aiming to serve abroad. In another example known to us, a company from the Far East operating in the UK, there was unease at the prospect of 55 year olds working on the conveyer belts. This was not ordinary ageism; rather it was a concern to avoid situations where the respect they would wish to give to older workers would be compromised.

The business case

Fairness issues stretch well beyond the treatment of ethnic minority groups and women. Being treated fairly is a basic human right and as such should be reflected in organizational policies on selection and assessment. This is important not only from a moral, but also a business point of view. For example, the way you handle your recruitment is strong PR for your organization. You do not want disaffected candidates bad-mouthing you, particularly in retail where every applicant is a potential customer. If you are in the UK and the Labour Party is in government when you read this, it is possible that civil rights legislation has already been enacted in which case selection and the fallout from it is bound to become a legal issue. For now it is a moral and business issue.

We have tried to ensure that fairness is considered throughout this book, reflecting our view of its central importance to recruitment and selection.

> **Skill requirement**
>
> Be able to demonstrate the fairness of your assessment processes in the wider sense.

SUMMARY

In this chapter we have outlined the context in which competency-based recruitment and selection must operate now, and in the near future, as we see it. In Chapter 2 we move on to critically discuss the building blocks of such a process – the competencies – and introduce you to Ros Fairburn of Fettercorn plc who is the leading light in our running case study.

REFERENCES

1. Drucker, P.F. (1992). *Managing for the Future.* Oxford: Butterworth Heinemann Ltd.
2. Hutton, W. (1994). *The State We're In.* Oxford: Basil Blackwell.
3. Bridges, W. (1995). *Job Shift.* London: Nicholas Brealey.
4. Lawler, E.E. (1993). From job-based to competency-based organizations. *Journal of Organisational Behaviour,* **15**, 3–15.
5. Herriot, P. and Pemberton C. (1995). *New Deals – The Revolution in Managerial Careers.* Chichester: Wiley.
6. Adapted from Herriot and Pemberton.
7. Coré, F. (1994). Women and the restructuring of employment. *The OECD Observer,* No. 186, February/March, 64.
8. Kandola, R.S. and Fullerton, J. (1994). *Managing the Mosaic: Diversity in Action.* London: Institute of Personnel and Development.
9. Payne, T. (1995). Editorial: Testing people with disabilities. *International Journal of Selection and Assessment,* **3**, 205–206.
10. Alkhader, O., Anderson N. and Clarke D. (1994). Computer-based testing: A review of recent developments in research and practice. *European Work and Organizational Psychologist,* **4**, 169–187.
11. Bartram, D. (1995). Guest editorial: computer-based testing. *International Journal of Selection and Assessment,* **3**, 73–74.
12. Whiddett, S., Payne, T. and Kandola, R.S. (1995). Organizational preferences: are public and private sector organizations perceived differently as potential employers? *Occupational Psychology Conference Book of Proceedings,* 202–211.
13. Anderson, N.R., Cunningham-Snell, N.A. and Haigh, J. (1996). Induction training as socialization: Current practice and attitudes to evaluation in British organizations. *International Journal of Selection and Assessment,* **4**, 169–184.
14. Sik, G. (1997). NASTY but nice ... *Selection and Development Review,* **13**, 16.
15. Wood, R. (1997). Credibility: a tricky test for publishers. *Personnel Today,* 13 February, 1997.
16. Baldry, C. and Fletcher, C. (1997). The integrity of integrity testing. *Selection and Development Review,* **13**, 3–6.
17. Lunn, T. (1995). Selecting and developing talent; an alternative approach. *Management Development Review,* **8**, 7–10.
18. Ancona, D.G. (1992). Demography and design: predictors of new product teams' performance. *Organization Science,* **3**, 321–341.
19. Kandola, R.S. and Fullerton, J. (1994). *Managing the Mosaic: Diversity in Action.* London: Institute of Personnel and Development.

Competencies: nothing new under the sun   2

Our objective in this chapter is to critically evaluate the notion of competencies. Whilst we are quite content for the time being to go along with the view that competencies are a useful tool for the personnel practitioner, particularly when used as a strategic tool to integrate HR processes, we think it important to set out the assumptions, limitations and possible implications of using the competency approach for recruitment and selection.

FETTERCORN plc – A CASE STUDY

Ros Fairburn stood up from her desk and moved over to the window. She had made a decision – this year Fettercorn was going into competency-based recruitment. She felt relieved now the decision had been made: excited, yes, but also a little anxious. Her experience at her last company told her what would be involved. The benefits were considerable, but so was the amount of work required – and the potential for disaster!

Before she could do anything, however, Ros knew she first had to sell the concept to Lupita, her boss and the MD of Fettercorn. Lupita was pretty hard nosed when it came to this sort of thing and was well known for being sceptical about what she called 'airy fairy HR fads and fancies'. Ros would need to have her facts straight before she tried to sell something as 'airy fairy' as competencies.

Ros walked back to her desk and sat down. She logged on to the Web and typed 'competencies and or competences' into her Web browser. She began to do some serious research . . .

THE STARTING POINT – WHAT DO WE WANT TO MEASURE?

In any book about recruitment and selection, competency-based or other-wise, there should be only one place to begin, and that is with the question: what do we want to measure? What is it about people that we want to investigate? Against what criteria can we evaluate candidates? A favourite answer to this question at the minute is 'competencies'.

Gone are the days, for most organizations at least, when candidates were called in for an 'informal chat' with a manager. Often, the manager would have no clear idea of what he or she was looking for – which characteristics of a person would distinguish the candidate who would go on to perform well in the job from the ones who would do badly. Typically, the manager would be interested in 'the cut of their jib', if they were made of 'the right stuff', if they 'had what it takes', or whether they would 'fit in'. This was probably as clear an idea as they had. The interview was, as we say, 'unstructured'.

It would be idle to pretend that these interviews no longer happen, especially in small organizations, but otherwise we have come a long way to the point where few large organizations would even think of starting a recruitment exercise without first defining their criteria. Even given the ongoing and impending changes sketched in Chapter 1 – the demise of the clearly defined job, and the need for adaptability and learning ability – it is still essential to know what we are looking for. Without clear criteria, we are left with the forlorn hope that 'I'll know it when I see it'. Not only is this unlikely to be true, but it is likely to lead to the selection of people similar to the interviewers. The research evidence here at least is strong: left to our own devices we tend to select people who we like, and we like people who are like us, in background, personality, appearance and style. This maintenance of the status quo, or 'cloning', will lead to a reduction in diversity – different views, styles, and approaches – and a loss of innova-tion potential within the organization[1]. The organization which reproduces itself runs the risk of becoming stale and arid. Not only that, but without clear criteria, it is impossible to defend selection decisions, particularly against the claims of unfair discrimination.

Whatever methods we use to assess people for selection and recruit-ment, we need a very clear idea of what type of person we are looking for. Having clear criteria, whether that means competencies or something else, is crucial.

WHAT ARE COMPETENCIES?

But what are competencies? In unpacking the concept, we propose to explore the following issues:

- the purposes of competencies
- Boyatzis and the birth of competencies
- modern competency frameworks
- challenges to the competency movement.

In doing so, we wish to draw the reader's attention to what we consider to be a worrying trend – the progressive simplification and muddying of the concept. It appears to us that the competency frameworks used today in organizations differ significantly from what was originally intended, both in nature and purpose. This is not necessarily serious, but the point needs to be made.

Although we use the word 'competencies' in this book, many organizations we have had contact with prefer to use more neutral terms. There are good reasons for this. To invite an unsuccessful candidate to come back with, 'So you are saying I'm incompetent?' would be most unfortunate. So other terms have come into play including 'capabilities' (but this invites the 'incapable' charge), 'standards of performance', 'critical success factors', 'criteria', 'dimensions', 'traits', or just 'abilities'. In our experience, these names all function in the same way – as summaries of behaviour which are useful to the extent that the user can derive value from them. The point about that – and it is reflected in our chapter title – is that there have always been names for bundles of like behaviours. Psychologists have been very accustomed to talking about abilities, traits or dimensions. Competencies are but the latest manifestation.

THE PURPOSES OF COMPETENCIES

Why have so many organizations introduced competency frameworks? Each year the journal *Competency* surveys a number of organizations to identify benchmarks and trends[2]. For 1996, the top 10 reasons for introducing competencies are shown in Box 2.1.

Evidently, competency frameworks are seen to serve many purposes. We must remember this when critiquing the concept.

The first thing to notice is that competencies are not seen as obvious vehicles for recruitment and selection (only the fourth highest priority purpose in the survey). It is what else they can do which seems to matter,

BOX 2.1   THE PURPOSE OF COMPETENCIES

- Performance
- Culture change
- Training and development
- Recruitment and selection
- Business objectives/competitiveness
- Career/succession planning
- Skills analysis
- Flexibility
- Clarity of role
- Integrating HR strategy.

especially when it comes to implementing a harmonized company-wide HR strategy. If you recruit people using a competency-based method, they and their managers can be given an indication of specific areas of strength and areas for development. This can link in to the performance management, or appraisal system, which in turn will provide evidence for succession planning, and even perhaps pay awards. Further competency-based assessment when in role can provide more detailed evidence on which areas the person needs to develop.

Competencies, then, offer a way of binding together and integrating the elements of a progressive human resources strategy. If competencies are defined, as they should be, with reference to the needs of the business, then a competency-based appraisal system can help to reinforce particular approaches to work (for example, continuous improvement or customer focus). Delivered in this way, competencies can be a powerful tool when trying to change the culture of an organization. The overall effect is to oblige everyone in the organization to focus on their performance in specific, common areas, to develop their skills accordingly, and ultimately to improve the performance of the organization.

The benefits of competencies in recruitment and selection

Whilst it may not be immediately obvious that competencies have a purpose in recruitment and selection, the benefits are nevertheless there:

- Experience with a range of organizations shows they improve our accuracy in assessing people's suitability or potential for different jobs.

- They facilitate a closer match between a person's skills and interests and the demands of the job.

- They help prevent interviewers and assessors from making 'snap' judgements about people or from judging them on characteristics that are irrelevant to the job in question.

- They can be used to underpin and structure the full range of assessment and development techniques – application forms, interviews, tests, assessment centres and appraisal ratings.

- By disaggregating an individual's profile into specific skills and characteristics, development plans can more accurately be targeted to areas of true development need.

The rest of the book is devoted to demonstrating how these claims work out in practice, but first we have to consider where the notion of competence came from. After that we will need to engage in a general discussion of the efficacy and limitations of the competency approach.

BOYATZIS AND THE BIRTH OF COMPETENCIES

What did we do BC (Before Competencies)? How did we recruit and select people for jobs, or assess them for promotion? Judging by the ubiquity of competencies today, anyone would think that selection and recruitment was a shambles BC. Not so. Before competency analysis and competencies, there was job analysis and criteria, or 'dimensions'. Commonly, personnel professionals or occupational psychologists would develop a job description including the key tasks and responsibilities involved and then from that hypothesise the skills, abilities, experience and personal attributes required of a successful job holder. The selection process was then built around this 'person specification'. This approach is still current – we do it ourselves – even with organizations who say they have an integrated competency-based HR system.

It is no accident that the concept of competencies grew out of the pressures on organizations to make themselves more effective through selecting, developing and rewarding the right people. It was in the context of managerial assessment that the American, Richard Boyatzis, first coined the term 'competencies'. His book, *The Competent Manager: A Model for Effective Performance*[3], laid down the agenda for the competency debate to follow.

Boyatzis' book is an eloquent work, blending persuasive economic argument with good quality applied research. For him, the competence of managers in the US economy was paramount. Page one of the book declares, 'It is the competence of managers that determines, in large part, the return that organizations realize from their human capital, or human resources'.

Boyatzis realized that when we select a manager, we have a model in our minds of what a 'good manager' looks like. All too often this is unconscious, or implicit; we are not fully aware of our model, and we may not have thought it out or explored it. Our model may be related to ourselves – our own characteristics – or to previous successful recruits, or even just 'the way it is' in the company. What is important is that, without realizing it, we are selecting managers by comparing their 'fit' to our mental model when our model may bear no relation to the personal characteristics required for the role.

Boyatzis' answer to the problem of poorly thought-out mental models of management was based on the methods of job analysis used by the staff of McBer and Company in the States, called the Job Competence Assessment Method. This is basically a behaviourally based interview technique (together with some projective tests) which rests on the comparison of the behaviours exhibited by current highly effective staff to the behaviours exhibited by less effective or even ineffective staff, where the behaviours are identified through the examination of critical incidents.

Boyatzis' hypothesis was that there are a certain fixed number of 'competencies' on which people can vary. As such, his work on competencies represents an alternative theoretical perspective on the study of individual differences at work. He quotes with approval Klemp's definition[4] of a competence:

> an underlying characteristic of a person which results
> in effective and/or superior performance in a job.

Thus, to Boyatzis, competencies are real aspects of human beings. Just as to Cattell (the author of 16PF) there are 16 personality traits, to Boyatzis people can be described in terms of 21 competencies. These are shown in Table 2.1.

Unlike many of his successors, Boyatzis intended the concept of competencies to be both rich and detailed. Each set of data gathered was analyzed to identify the characteristics which superior performers possessed. These were clustered into common themes and given a title, a definition and a list of behaviours which would signal the presence or absence of the competency. While so many modern competency frameworks are exclusively concerned with 'observable behaviour', reflecting the dominance of behaviourism in occupational psychology and, by extension, HR practice, Boyatzis was concerned to include a wider range of psychological aspects in his model. In particular, he specified three

Goal and Action Management Cluster	Directing Subordinates Cluster
Efficiency orientation Productivity Diagnostic use of concepts Concern with impact	Developing others Use of unilateral power Spontaneity
Leadership Cluster	Focus on Other Clusters
Self-confidence Use of oral presentations Logical thought Conceptualization	Self-control Perceptual objectivity Stamina and adaptability Concern with close relationships
Human Resource Cluster	Specialised Knowledge
Use of socialized power Positive regard Managing group processes Accurate self-assessment	Memory Specialized knowledge

Table 2.1   Boyatzis' 21 Competencies

levels of a competency, which he said would 'affect different aspects of the individual's application of a particular competency in a job' (p. 28). The three levels were:

- motive and trait
- self-image and social role
- skill.

Boyatzis identified these three components for each competence. For example, someone who had a high efficiency orientation would be *motivated* primarily by a high need for achievement, would have a *self-image* of 'I can do better' and 'I am efficient', might take a *social role* such as 'innovator', and might exhibit observable *skills* such as 'goal-setting, planning and organizing resources efficiently'.

Someone with a high concern for impact may be *motivated* by a need for power, may have a *self-image* which says 'I am important', may prefer to take on *social roles* which are associated with status, and may exhibit observable *skills* such as influencing behaviour.

By identifying and exploring competencies at these three levels, Boyatzis was involved in building up a rich psychological picture of a person –

one which can explain why someone behaves in the way they do, and can predict how they will behave in certain situations (the basic goals of all good science). This richness has certainly been lost in many modern competency frameworks.

An alternative to Boyatzis: competences used to define minimum standards

Boyatzis' approach to competencies was driven by the need to make corporations more effective through selecting, developing and rewarding the right people. As such, it concentrated on identifying the characteristics of superior performers. In the UK, the government has taken a different approach guided by a different objective – to raise the minimum standards of performance at work nationally. While Boyatzis focused on internal characteristics of a person, the British government, through the medium of the National Council for Vocational Qualifications (NCVQ), has focused on defining the tasks and outcomes required of the job. These are often referred to as competen*ces*, rather than competen*cies*. Making this distinction can easily descend into nitpicking but inasmuch as there are differences between the two, Table 2.2 sets them out.

	Competencies	Competences
Origin	USA	UK
Purpose	Identify superior performers	Identify minimum standards
Focus	The person	The job/role
Summary of ...	Personal characteristics	Tasks/outputs
Target	Managers	Everyone, but less so managers

Table 2.2   Competencies versus Competences[5]

In what follows, we shall concentrate on the US version – competen*cies* – that is, emphasising the person and personal characteristics as a route to superior performance.

MODERN COMPETENCY FRAMEWORKS

We noted that modern competency frameworks, where organizations have used the Boyatzis approach, have tended to simplify the concept, focusing only on the observable behaviour (in Boyatzis' terms, skill level). Driven more by practical necessity and the need to generate ownership and buy-in than by any coherent theoretical argument, organizations have resorted to an eclectic approach to competency definition. As a result, frameworks often include a mixture of behaviours, values, tasks, aspirations and personality characteristics.

Again drawing on the *Competency* journal survey, we can identify the 12 most commonly adopted competencies, as cited by a sample of UK organizations. We chose the top 12 as the evidence indicates that the most common number of competencies arrived at is between eight and twelve, although there is great variation between organizations. Box 2.2 has the results.

BOX 2.2   THE 12 MOST COMMON COMPETENCIES

- Communication
- Achievement/results orientation
- Customer focus
- Teamwork
- Leadership
- Planning and organizing
- Commercial/business awareness
- Flexibility/adaptability
- Developing others
- Problem solving
- Analytical thinking
- Building relationships.

That there is a mixture is plain. Achievement/results orientation, problem solving and analytical thinking stem from Boyatzis, being clearly 'internal characteristics' of a person. The same cannot be said for customer focus and commercial/business awareness, which are much more experiential and context-dependent.

Close study of Box 2.2 will show that these twelve competencies fall naturally into three groups. Moreover, the three groups correspond to the old tripartite system, known to the ancient Greeks, of thinking, feeling and acting (cognitive, affective and conative). If you have to reduce 30 or so competencies to a manageable number – and we have often had to do this for organizations – then working in terms of thinking, feeling (or relating), and acting is as good a way of proceeding as any. Interestingly, a survey of what 'future top managers', i.e. high flyers, expect of themselves (and what their personnel directors expect of them) named *leadership, communication skills,* and *strategic thinking* as the most important qualities[6]. These, of course, correspond to acting, feeling and thinking or, if you wish, to acting/feeling, feeling/thinking, and thinking.

Only the purist would harp on about competency lists being mongrels. Unless there is a better explanation, we have to believe that these schemes evolve the way they do because they serve a purpose for organizations in mobilizing employees to focus their efforts in the same direction. In that respect, you could say that competencies are a statement of what the human capital of the business is meant to achieve. When, in 1996, and after seven years, one of our clients revisited its competencies, it found that the business had moved on in such a way that it was now necessary to define competencies which would reflect a new-found emphasis on developing people and managing change.

It is instructive to take a competency apart. Table 2.3 does this for a typical competency – planning and organizing.

Title	Planning and organizing
Definition	The ability to visualize a sequence of actions needed to achieve a goal and to estimate the resources required. A preference for acting in a structured, thorough manner.
Indicators	*Level 1 – junior manager* • manages own time and personal activities • breaks complex activities into manageable tasks • identifies possible obstacles to planned achievement. *Level 2 – middle manager* • produces contingency plans for possible future occurrences • estimates in advance the resources and time scales needed to meet objectives • co-ordinates team activities to make the best use of individual skills and specialisms. *Level 3 – senior manager* • identifies longer term operational implications of business plans • effectively plans utilisation of all resources.

Table 2.3 A Competency in Detail

The table demonstrates the four key aspects of the modern competency – title, definition, behavioural indicators, and a levelling mechanism. There are many variations on this theme, but in essence this is what a competency should look like. Note that the behavioural indicators are absolutely key. Without them it would be impossible to assess people objectively against a competency.

CHALLENGES TO THE COMPETENCY MOVEMENT

As protagonist in a debate at the 1996 British Psychological Society Occupational Psychology Conference, our colleague, Binna Kandola, organized his critique of competencies around the following allusions:

- living in the past
- irreconcilable differences
- a shoddy job
- cloning
- it's difficult to turn a tanker.

Living in the past

The techniques used to identify competencies, notably behaviourally based interviews, critical incident and repertory grid interviews, share one serious flaw. They help us identify the characteristics of people who have been successful *up to now*. They say nothing about what people will need in the future. The danger is that organizations will use competency frameworks to shape their futures based on what worked in the past. The chances are they will be wrong. As Paul Sparrow has said, it is like 'trying to drive ahead whilst looking in the rear-view mirror'[7].

One way to face up to this problem is, as Steven Covey has urged[8], to begin with the end in mind. We gave the example of our client re-shaping its future. If you want a process, imagine a visioning exercise where board members are asked to take their five-year strategic objectives and identify which behaviours their managers will need to produce if those goals are to be attained. Next, imagine that the top team is tasked to come up with a list of behaviours which are then clustered to provide a first cut competency framework. Such a framework is bound to contain some of the 'typical' competencies which always crop up, and which we saw earlier, but there will be some that are startlingly different; for example:

- learning to learn

- learning from mistakes
- managing diversity effectively.

Of course that is only the beginning of the process, as the draft framework must be checked out, refined and validated with the managers themselves. Beginning with the end in mind, however, certainly helps to break some paradigms. It also ensures that the competency framework does not itself become the objective, and the purpose for which it is going to be used is kept clearly in focus.

Irreconcilable differences

When done correctly, behavioural event and critical incident interviews compare highly effective and less effective staff with a view to surfacing the differentiating characteristics. But there are dangers in this. Some differences may be irrelevant; some of the things which do not differentiate may nevertheless be important; and there will be characteristics that none of the successful people have, but which the organization needs or, more likely, will need. It is also possible that the variables that differentiate the two groups have nothing to do with performance, but merely reflect stereotypes or assumptions of the organizational culture. As an example, we recently came across a competency framework which contained an indicator which stated baldly: 'is under thirty'. Believe it or not, this was included as an indicator of analytical ability. The organization felt once employees were over 30 they were no longer capable of thinking quickly enough to do the job. The indicator was thrown up because in the samples used in the job analysis analytical skill happened to correlate inversely with age. In fact, age had (and has) nothing to do with the competency or with performance on the job and has a complex relationship with cognitive function. To have applied the indicator as a criterion would have caused unfair discrimination on age grounds, and although not yet illegal, would have had the effect of screening out many able applicants.

The key practical step to minimizing such problems is to use a variety of approaches to competency identification, choosing from different types of interviews, focus groups, visioning exercises as described earlier, consultation sessions and questionnaires.

A shoddy job

We will not beat about the bush – many of the competency frameworks designed for organizations are poor. It starts with too many, far too many, competencies. One organization came up with 390, yes as few as that! Guess for yourself whether the system was being used. It had collapsed under its own weight.

An equally serious problem is the quality of the behavioural indicators. These can be inconsistently written, misleading, impossible to measure, or downright discriminatory, as we just saw. Indicators can also be poorly classified. For example, does the indicator 'asks people's opinions' belong in: (i) team working, (ii) interpersonal skills, (iii) communication, (iv) influencing, or (v) leading? The greater the difficulty classifying indicators, the less useful the competencies. As an aid to writing behavioural indicators, we have produced a check list (see Box 2.3).

BOX 2.3   A CHECK LIST FOR BEHAVIOURAL INDICATORS[9]

Each indicator should:

- describe directly observable behaviour, or other specific evidence of an individual's competency
- describe just one piece of behaviour or evidence
- not be duplicated under two or more competencies
- include a verb phrase, i.e. describe action
- include enough contextual information to make the action meaningful
- be fair.

Cloning

This is a favourite theme of Binna Kandola[10]. The danger of identifying who is performing their job well, and then selecting more just like them, is that we end up with clones. Why is that a problem? Well, although the jury is still out[11], it seems likely that if you reduce the diversity in your organization, or more likely fail to expand it, you also reduce the creativity, capacity for innovation, diversity of approaches, problem solving skills, etc. In short, the organization can stagnate. It has often been observed that if organizations do not innovate, they die. Binna Kandola believes that we need to place far less emphasis on the detailed descriptions of the ways in which we would like people to work. Instead, we should make clear the organizational values, each person's objectives, then allow them to work within those parameters.

As we shall discuss later in Chapter 4, the difference between competencies and values is a matter of degree, and if you are to use values for any tangible HR process, then behavioural indicators will be necessary, which further breaks down the distinction. Nevertheless, in this sense, values can be seen as the guiding but not defining or over-specifying how we can and should behave. They should perhaps set the boundaries of unacceptable behaviour, but leave the possibilities of acceptable behaviour up to the imaginations of our talented staff.

It's difficult to turn a tanker

Competency frameworks can be powerful things. If they are being used as the basis for all recruitment and selection, development and reward, pretty soon people will get the message and begin to exhibit the behaviours that are being reinforced. There is a problem with this. By the time people have begun to change, the market may have moved; the skill requirements are different, and the competencies required of managers have also changed. This means at the very least a review of the competency framework, at the most a complete project to define a new set. Who wants that sort of hassle every two years? The upshot is that many competency frameworks in use are out of date, yet have become embedded in the bureaucracy, which means they are liable to be counterproductive. The implications are that competency frameworks must be closely monitored and, occasionally, revised.

PROBLEMS RELATING TO RECRUITMENT AND SELECTION

Having had the general discussion, we can get back to recruitment and selection. It is possible to pick out three basic assumptions underlying competency-based selection and recruitment which do not necessarily hold up under challenge:

- Observable behaviour is all that is important – feelings and emotions are not important.

This is an echo of our point that competencies today have become over simplified. OK, observable behaviours are important, but they are not everything. How we feel when faced with a setback; the state of our motivation when faced with two competing tasks – we cannot necessarily observe these things but they are important. This is evidenced by assessors at assessment centres who, despite thorough training instructing them to be objective, and 'call it as you see it', still manage to justify their conclusions with guesses about the internal makeup of the candidate.

- Competencies are not compensatory – to succeed in organizations, a person should have them all.

It is sometimes supposed that, to be successful, a candidate must demonstrate competence throughout the framework. This is almost certainly naïve. Occasionally someone will come along who seems to score uniformly highly, but even they will have some strengths and some weaknesses. The norm is that people will have mixed profiles. That should not be so surprising. Clive Fletcher has pointed out that when we analyze competencies in psychological terms, they often do not make sense: 'Either the psychological qualities required for different behaviours described under a single competency conflict with each other, or the same thing is true across two (or more) different competencies – implying that it is unlikely that an individual could score highly on both'[12]. This is an argument we have no difficulty signing up to as it echoes one of our own alternative approaches to assessment (see Box 2.4).

- It is possible to distinguish an individual's contribution from that of the team; it is possible to correctly attribute skill and success.

How many times have you stopped an interviewee to ask the question: 'Excuse me, you said "we" made that decision. Who is "we"? What was *your* role?' only to get the answer 'it was a team decision – we all contributed equally.' Although such an answer makes it difficult to mark the interview, it may well be true. So much of our work in organizations today is conducted in teams that it may no longer be possible to attribute specific skills, abilities or even outcomes to individuals. Perhaps we need to assess the competency of 'a team' rather than individuals. Perhaps it is time for occupational psychologists to learn from clinical psychologists that it is not just the individual's characteristics which determine how well they perform, but the environment in which they work – the opportunities they are given and the way they are rewarded. Team-based assessment does not sound such a bad idea.

SUMMARY

In this chapter, we have critically examined the notion of competencies – their history and their present incarnations. It will be apparent, from the nature of the beast, that competencies are not perfect as criteria for selection and recruitment. They are based on assumptions which may not always stand up; they can be unwieldy; they may not promote diversity; they have become simplified to the point of banality given where Boyatzis started; and, finally, they have become an end in themselves rather than a means to an end, as the competency industry grinds on. Yet, imperfect though they are, competencies have many operational benefits, whether strategic or pragmatic. In particular, they can provide a sort of road map for where the business wants to go, and what behaviours and actions are going to be needed. Those who can see the force of this argument will have no difficulty agreeing that it makes sense to build recruitment and selection processes around competency frameworks, flawed though they may be. In what follows, we show how to do this from beginning to end.

BOX 2.4   PSYCHOLOGICAL ASSESSMENT: AN ALTERNATIVE APPROACH TO COMPETENCIES?

In the course of our work, we are often involved in individual psychological assessments, usually for senior managers or executives. In this work, we take a more deliberately psychological approach. Specifically, we are concerned with measuring the psychological characteristics of intellect, personality and motivation, rather than the competencies themselves, for it is the expression of these characteristics in combination which manifest in competencies. In that respect, we are digging below the surface.

For example, *planning and organizing* is about how well we can use the various psychological characteristics; does our intellect allow us to think through the implications of actions; are we motivated to choose to put our energy into planning as opposed to getting stuck straight in to the task; is our personality such that we will respond in a constructive and optimistic way when problems occur; are our problem-solving skills good enough to remove these obstacles; does our personality allow us to abandon previous courses of action to which we had committed ourselves, and to find a new way forward? In our view, to talk about planning and organizing as if it is something we automatically 'have' is wrong – it is about how we harness and apply our core characteristics (combined of course with any specific skills, e.g. in this case, use of planning software or Gantt charts) in the world of work.

FETTERCORN plc – A CASE STUDY

Ros scanned the faces of Lupita and the other directors, looking for a hint of acceptance, resistance, anything.

'That concludes my presentation on competencies and competency-based recruitment. I think we can agree that whilst there are some drawbacks to such an approach, if we do it properly and get some good advice, the benefits could be considerable.'

She sat down and waited for the inevitable grilling . . .

Lupita smiled and shook Ros's hand. 'I like it. It's simple and it's going to work,' she said. 'The thing that really sold it to me was the distinction between thinking, feeling, and acting. It just makes intuitive sense. And I think you're right – we should use it for the Head Buyer recruitment coming up in the new year. It's vital we get that appointment right. Congratulations, Ros, and good luck.'

'Good luck is right,' thought Ros, as she leaned against the wall of the lift. The new Head Buyer had to be in place before the end of March, and it was already December. That was not a long time. At least she already had the makings of a competency framework – the legacy of a consultancy project commissioned by her predecessor but never used. The framework was pretty standard and it fitted into the tripartite model. That should keep Lupita happy, at least.

Ros made it back to her desk and sat down. 'Better do some planning,' she said to herself.

THE FETTERCORN COMPETENCY FRAMEWORK

Thinking
- Analysis
- Learning ability

Feeling
- Influencing
- Interpersonal skills

Acting
- Planning and organizing
- Achievement drive.

Thinking

Analysis

Identifies information to analyse, and applies reasoning skills to help inform decisions.

- Identifies information required for analysis
- Identifies patterns and themes in data
- Uses both 'hard' and 'soft' data for analysis
- Demonstrates inductive and deductive reasoning
- Makes objective decisions based on analysis.

Learning ability

The desire to continually learn and improve own knowledge and understanding. Takes learning opportunities and learns quickly.

- Learns from their mistakes
- Learns new techniques/processes rapidly
- Identifies and takes opportunities to learn
- Learns in a variety of ways, e.g. from experience, books, people, etc.
- Prepared to change approach in the light of experience.

Feeling

Influencing

The ability to win people around to their way of thinking, using logical fact-based argument and persuasive skills and tactics.

- Identifies the key people to influence
- Identifies the needs and wants of those to be influenced
- Uses logical argument based on fact when persuading
- Uses tactics, such as involving people, tailoring the message, or bargaining
- Presents counter arguments in a constructive, neutral way.

Interpersonal skills

Empathizes with others, and respects people as individuals. Balances the need to be directive and consultative when required.

- Listens actively to others
- Values differences and treats people with respect
- Uses appropriate non-verbal/body language
- Communicates own needs/feelings in a clear way
- Does not react defensively/take things personally.

Acting

Planning and organizing

The ability to visualize a sequence of actions needed to achieve a goal and to estimate the resources required. A preference for acting in a structured, thorough manner.

- manages own time and personal activities
- breaks complex activities into manageable tasks
- identifies possible obstacles to planned achievement
- produces contingency plans for possible future occurrences
- estimates in advance the resources and time scales needed to meet objectives.

Achievement drive

The motivation and drive to achieve results and get things done. A preference for persistence and resilience.

- is proactive at identifying areas in which to add value
- completes tasks set to time/budget/quality
- finds ways around problems/setbacks
- volunteers for extra tasks/duties
- inspires others to put in extra effort.

REFERENCES

1. Herriot, P. and Anderson, N.R. (1997). Selecting for change: How will personnel and selection psychology survive? In Anderson, N.R. and Herriot, P. (Eds) *International Handbook of Selection and Assessment*. Chichester: Wiley, 1997.
2. Matthewman, J. (1996) Trends and developments in the use of competency frameworks. *Competency*, **4**, 1, 2–11.
3. Boyatzis, R.E. (1982). *The Competent Manager: A Model for Effective Performance*. New York: John Wiley.
4. Klemp, G.O. Jr. (1980). *The assessment of occupational competence*. Report to the National Institute of Education, Washington, DC.
5. Adapted from Tool 1 of the Tools for assessment and development centres, Whiddett, S. (1996). *Tools for assessment and development centres*. London: Institute for Personnel and Development; and from Adams, K. (1996). Competency comes of age. *Competency*, **4**, 1, 25–32.
6. GHN (1994). *Future Top Manager's Report*. London: GHN.
7. Sparrow, P. (1997). *Organizational competencies: A valid approach for the future?* In Anderson, N.R. and Herriot, P. (Eds) *International Handbook of Selection and Assessment*. Chichester: Wiley, 1997.
8. Covey, S.R. (1995). *Living the seven habits: Applications and insights*. London: Simon & Schuster Audio.
9. Whiddett, S. (1996). *Tools for assessment and development centres*. London: Institute for Personnel and Development.
10. Kandola, R.S. (1996). Putting competencies in perspective. *Competency*, **4**, 1, 31–34.
11. Kandola, R.S. and Fullerton, J. (1994). *Managing the Mosaic: Diversity in Action*. Institute for Personnel and Development, London.
12. Fletcher, C. (1996). Mix and match fails to work on competencies. *People Management*, 12 September, 53–54.

Designing the selection process as a whole   3

In this chapter we encourage the idea of looking at the selection process as a whole. We illustrate what a process might look like overall, from start to finish, and identify the key decisions which must be made up-front. We show how different combinations of assessment methods may be more or less appropriate depending on factors such as numbers of applicants, costs, predictive power of the methods, etc. We also look at the key question of sequencing of methods, as well as issues of planning and resource availability which will determine the specifics of the process.

FETTERCORN plc – A CASE STUDY

Ros knew that the decision to run with a competency-based system was just the first of many. For example, where should she advertise? What should she put and not put, in the ad? Should she ask for a CV, or send an application form, or both? Did she need one or two interviews? What would be the implications of using some psychometrics? Where would those fit best, before or after the interview(s)? And should she use an assessment centre to help make the final appointment decision? That could really stretch the budget.

The answers to these questions depended on many parameters, but especially time scales, budget, and projected number of applicants. Ros knew that a mistake at this stage could have big consequences, so she had decided to get some outside help. She had invited a consultant – Jack Connelly – to make a presentation on how he could make her life easier, and help answer some of her questions.

'Good morning, Jack. Glad you could make it. Come on in.' Jack shook her hand and began to set up his laptop for the presentation. Ros sat down, saying 'Whenever you're ready, take it away.' (She had met Jack before, when he had credentialized himself and his company.) 'OK,' said Jack. 'As I see it, these are the issues you are going to have to face ... '

THE SELECTION PROCESS AS AN ENTITY

In any serious recruitment drive, the key questions for the recruiter always turn out to be (in no particular order of importance except that they are all important):

- how much money do you have to spend?

- what methods will you use?

- in what order?

- who will be the assessors?

- are they trained?

- how long do you have?

- how many people do you want to recruit?

- how many applications do you expect?

- into what functions? can there be a common process?

- do you want or need external help? where can it add value most?

- how are you going to give information, as well as get it?

- how are you going to project the organization to applicants?

- what are you going to do to treat applicants and candidates well?

For example, if you are on a tight budget, then you may need to forget about assessment centres; if you are expecting, on the basis of experience, 5000 application forms, then you had better make sure you have an effective screening mechanism worked out in advance; if you need some-one in place in three weeks' time, then a multi-stage recruitment process is a non-starter. In formulating answers to these questions, it pays to think in terms of the whole selection process, from start to finish. Piecemeal or quick fix solutions invariably unravel because of unwanted knock-on effects. As we shall see (Chapter 9), assessment centres provide a good example, in microcosm, of what is involved in co-ordinating a selection process.

Looking at the process as a whole is actually quite novel. Research has tended to focus on the separate components of a selection process, such as 'the interview' or 'the personality profile'. As a result, the moving parts have been given a lot of attention but quite where to put them, and what the effect will be of putting that next to that, has not always been appreciated. It is possible to address this issue knowledgeably and systematically, and that is what we will do now.

Before that, we might just marvel that we can talk about a 'process' at all, about there being several methods involved, and about there being several stages to it. The first author secured his first meaningful job via an interview conducted during his lunch break on a park bench in the gardens adjoining the Tower of London. The second author much more recently, has experienced (and benefited from) what a multi-stage process can do (Box 6.1: Chapter 6). Thankfully, there has been a sea change in the way we recruit and select people, and it has been all to the good.

Not that you would bet your mortgage on the old practices having disappeared completely. In fact, they haven't. Take the method of selecting British Members of Parliament – a meeting of the constituency association, at which the candidates make speeches and answer questions, followed by the decision. How many constituency associations saddled with MPs accused of 'sleaze' must be kicking themselves that they did not put their Member through more hoops. This is a classic example of what happens when one aspect of the job analysis – the perceived need for the 'gift of the gab' – is allowed to dominate or even over-ride the others.

BANG FOR THE BUCK

A useful term in selection is 'utility'; in the vernacular, bang for the buck. Among some academics it is under a cloud at the moment[1], either because they have lost confidence in their ability to calculate it, or because they think no one pays attention anyway. But it remains a helpful way of evaluating the worth of selection methods, even if no one quite has the stomach for working through the equations.

The utility of a particular selection method, e.g. the interview, depends crucially on: (i) how valid it is (how well it predicts future job performance), and (ii) how expensive it is (which hinges on the numbers involved). There is a trade-off here, so that expensive but indisputably valid methods (assessment centres) may have greater utility than cheaper but less valid methods. We say 'may have' because cost and validity do not always march hand in hand. Take personality questionnaires. Because training is required to interpret the results, and because, generally speaking, they are more elaborate than ability tests (more pages, more scoring keys, more accompanying literature), personality questionnaires end up costing, as a rough rule of thumb, at least half as much again per test taker as an ability test (and that is not counting in the licensing fees which some test publishers charge). Yet, from everything we know, personality questionnaires are nowhere near as useful – on their own – as ability tests in predicting who will perform well.

That begs the question as to why you would use personality questionnaires at all. After all, you would not pay more for poorer food. The answer is that, in some circumstances, personality questionnaires will provide *incremental* validity over and above what ability tests, or anything else, will give. In particular, it has been suggested that relevant personality measures can provide significant incremental validity beyond that of the assessment centre and vice-versa[2]. We will come back to this in Chapter 9. For now we would say that if the outcome is supported by other work, then personality measures could have higher utility than assessment centres (Goffin, Rothstein and Johnston calculated that the cost of the assessment centre per candidate was 270 times higher than the personality measure). Now that really would put the cat among the pigeons!

A more general point to be made about the utility of personality measures is that usage is typically 'soft' rather than 'hard'. When using them in connection with personal development, utility hardly matters since no one bothers to work out the cost–benefit equation and if they did it would probably be infinitely elastic.

Ability tests score well on utility. In fact, of all the methods, ability tests used on their own offer the best trade-off between cost and validity. All studies agree that tests of general cognitive ability are good predictors of job and training performance when the job or training demands a high level of thought. The more complex the job or the training, the better tests work. With ability tests we can bracket *work sample tests*, which are known to produce predictive validities at least as high as conventional ability tests[3]. Because of these properties, and because they are relatively cheap, ability tests (or work samples) can be used towards the front end to screen out large numbers of candidates, leaving the more expensive (and valid) methods, i.e. assessment centres, for the final selection. That, at any rate, is the theory. In practice, as we shall see and as we know, it is the interview which invariably appears at the end of the process, a method which is reasonably cheap (although not if it is overdone) but whose validity, in the generality, inspires no great confidence.

EN BLOC OR SEQUENCED?

So far we have been talking as if the process was inevitably organized in stages, with applicant numbers decreasing at each stage. That is not always the case. There are selection processes where all applicants do everything, call this the *en bloc* process, and the more familiar *sequenced* process, with applicants dropping out at each stage.

En bloc processes

In the context of selection for employment, the en bloc process is probably quite rare (although the norm in other contexts e.g. school or college examinations), and rarer still when the applications are of an order of magnitude that can properly only be called 'mass'. We know of only one instance, and that was not strictly selection for employment directly, but selection to, as it were, pre-qualify for employment. This was the process for selecting people to train as barristers on the Bar Vocational Course run by the Inns of Court School of Law for three years from 1994 to 1996.

The point to make about this process is that it was driven entirely by equity principles. It does not seem to have crossed anyone's mind to do other than allow everyone to have the chance to show what they had to offer, specifically in terms of several sources of evidence structured around five competencies. The numbers of applicants were around 2200 in the first year, and around 1500 in the following years. The process thus could be seen as a kind of huge assessment centre. There was a scored application form targeted at all the competencies and that could have been used to whittle down the numbers, but what an outcry there would have been. And the same would have been true of any other single method. In other words, no one method of sifting could have been defended, especially and uniquely, given the players, ever ready to go to law themselves. There was, indeed, difficulty defending the whole process in its Mark I version[4].

In reality – and this is important – there was not a lot of sifting to do. In year one, just under two thirds of applicants were accepted on to the course, and in years two and three that proportion rose to more like four-fifths – not much selection at all. All that was going on was the exclusion of the 'definitely not up to it' applicants. In these circumstances a sequenced process would not have made much sense at all, although the Inns of Court could not have known that at the time. The process was in place before they knew how many applications they were going to get.

As a postscript to this account, consider what happened in 1997, the first year that institutions other than the Inns of Court School of Law have been allowed to offer the Bar Vocational Course. As we write, it was reported (*The Times*, March 20, 1997) that 1800 students applied for 120 places offered by the College of Law (another institution). Now that *will* mean selection. No details are available as to what process the College of Law used to find the 120. Our best guess would be degree class, where the degree was obtained, and the quality of the application form.

Needless to say, the trainee barrister selection process was not cheap. Just to give a flavour of it, in years two and three every applicant (1500 or so) was required to give a five minute oral presentation in front of two assessors, a barrister and a lay person with experience of administering the law. It is a good example of the validity–cost trade-off and, in particular, having to pay for validity. Validity was clearly enhanced by having a direct measure of advocacy, and also direct measures of writing skills (through three double-marked written exercises), but the costs were high, as they always are for direct measures, which is why indirect measures, notably tests, find favour.

Just as there was no acceptability at all among the legal fraternity for anyone being weeded out by any one method (or, if the truth be told, for anyone at all being weeded out), among people, in the generality, there is acceptance, grudging or otherwise, that an organization has to find some way of reducing a stack of applications to something manageable, and if that has to be done, first through the application form or CV and then by other methods, then so be it. They might go to law – perhaps they ought to go to law on occasion – but they do not.

Sequenced processes

We sometimes call a sequenced process a *designed-through* process. When one of us was working with the Employment Service and the Inland Revenue to revamp their recruitment practices, that was the term commonly used. In both processes there were three stages. First came a scored competency-based application form (like those shown in Chapter 5). This served to eliminate many applicants. The survivors were then asked to complete one or more work sample tests each tapping into a different competency (see Chapter 7). More applicants were rejected. Those that remained were given a structured interview, competency-based, of course (see Chapter 6). The candidates were then evaluated against their results on all three components, and final accept/reject decisions made. Advice was also offered on advertising, on phrasing a suitable rejection letter, and on how to feed back to disappointed candidates. That is competency-based recruitment from A to Z.

It will be obvious that the positioning of a selection method in a sequence affects both its predictive ability and its utility. Figure 3.1 (using made up but not unrealistic numbers, and where r is the validity coefficient) illustrates how the different stages of a selection process are interdependent, in that the latter stages in the process are fundamentally determined by the decisions taken earlier.

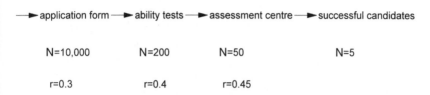

Figure 3.1   A Sequenced Recruitment and Selection Process

With the arrows go increasing restriction of range of ability, increasing cost of method, reduction in numbers, and increase in validity of method. Restriction of range can be overlooked, but in progressively refining the quality of the applicant pool, you are in fact making it more and more difficult to identify the best candidates. The implication of this is that the selection methods you use toward the end of the process must be capable of making fine-grain distinctions between very good candidates.

Deploying selection methods different in character as well as tapping into different competencies is likely – and certainly intended – to produce incremental validity at each stage. When this works, the system as a whole is said to possess *synergistic* validity[5]. The more the elements complement rather than replicate each other, the greater the synergistic validity. That said, as the methods become more valid they become more expensive (not necessarily the other way round as we saw with personality question-naires) so that ultimately there is a complex trade-off between cost, validity, number of candidates, and progressive restriction of the ability range. How much harder it is to select the top 10 from 100 applicants compared to the top 100 from 10,000!

DOESN'T IT GO AGAINST COMMON SENSE TO USE THE LEAST VALID METHODS FIRST?

Some will find it counter-intuitive that less valid methods should be put at the front end. Surely you want to minimize the number of good candidates who are screened out at the outset, and get rid of all the no-hopers. There are at least two answers to this. One is that you are most unlikely to lose the really excellent candidates even with a low validity screen. They are more or less guaranteed not to turn in a poor application form. And if you intend to appoint only a very few really excellent candidates, then it does not matter too much that you have lost some good candidates who, for whatever reason, have turned in a poor application form. As for those applicants who produce a good application form, and get past the first hurdle, but who are not what is wanted, they will almost certainly be excluded by the more valid methods which follow on.

Another answer hinges on what is meant by validity. This is a general point which we may as well open up here. The relationship between the predictor (selection process or individual methods) and what is being predicted (strong performance on the job) is not symmetrical or even, especially at the ends of the distributions. Even the most valid selection methods are less good at predicting who will be successful than who will definitely not be successful. That is even more true for the less valid methods. This means that all methods are better at finding those who ought to be excluded than at locating future stars. That is because there is a lot that goes into being a star that selection methods do not catch, or do not catch very well, like all those aspects of everyday judgement we call 'managerial nous'.

Some data from the Inns of Court School of Law selection process help to illustrate the effect the application form can have when used to screen. Table 3.1 shows the relationship between the predictor (application form score or AF) and the criterion (course grades on the Bar Vocational Course)*.

AF score	Fail	Competent	Very competent	Outstanding
Poor	52%	32%	16%	0%
Weak	30%	55%	14%	1%
Good	19%	53%	27%	1%
Very good	17%	49%	32%	2%

Table 3.1   Relationship of Application Form Scores to Course Grades

The table shows that there are very few 'Outstanding' candidates to start with (about 40), but if a 'Poor' score on the application form is taken to mean 'Discard', then none of them would have been screened out (had screening been in operation). Rather more 'Very competent' people (16%) would have been screened out but, as just noted, if only the 'Outstanding' people are wanted this does not matter. Then there are the 17% who managed a very good application form score, but failed the course. Naturally, that was a waste but had they been screened on, say, the first course grading, they might well have been discarded. Incidentally, the correlation between the application form score and the course total was

---

*   Thanks to the Council of Legal Education and to Charles Johnson for permission to use this table.

0.22, which would ordinarily be classed as low validity. So it just shows what is possible in these circumstances.

Selection methods also put a limit on what stars are allowed to produce. Think of a test – you can't do better than a perfect score. Failure, on the other hand, is failure, after allowances have been made for nerves etc. The upshot is that even the less valid methods, like the application form, will be reasonably efficient at sorting out those who won't make it. Knowing that, it must be the case that there are quantum improvements to be made in prediction by actually targeting the content and thrust of exercises on what makes people fail. Looking at Box 3.1, which is about what makes managers fail, it is easy to imagine selection methods picking up some of the success factors, but not too many of the derailing factors. Here is the real challenge for executive selection. Think of Members of Parliament as executives and you have it. How do you spot a sleazebag before he or she can do any damage?

BOX 3.1   WHY EXECUTIVES FAIL

Researchers at the Center for Creative Leadership in North Carolina[6] studying executives who failed, or in their terms were 'derailed', asked, 'Why was success predicted?', and got the answers:

- track record
- technical or business competence
- outgoing, charming
- loyalty to management
- willingness to lead.

Then they asked what were the reasons for derailment, and got these answers:

- decline in business performance
- insensitive, abrasive, intimidating style
- cold, aloof, arrogant
- betrayed trust
- over-managing
- poor at choosing staff
- overly ambitious

So, from different perspectives, it is possible to understand why it is not just acceptable to put the lower validity methods in first, but actually desirable. It would simply be a waste to kick off with a high validity method. There is a police force known to us which, after a paper sift to eliminate obviously unsuitable applicants, such as those with a criminal record, puts the rest, i.e. the great majority, through a half-day assessment centre. Those who get through this are then interviewed. Quite why they persist with a high validity method so early on in the process is not clear; it is only half a day and perhaps they benefit from economies of scale. What is significant is that they have been looking to experiment with an upgraded application form, and are also helping us to pilot a form for use by police forces nationally. They appear to have realized that more screening can and should be done with the application form before activating the assessment centre.

From what we have been saying, and the examples we have used, it would appear that the preferred sequence would be: application form/ CV, then some form of psychometrics (ability test(s)/work sample test(s)/personality questionnaire), followed either by an interview or interviews, or by an assessment centre.

Unfortunately, perfectly rational processes like the one described above are too often compromised by ending the process with an interview. The (un)desirability of finishing with an interview is something we have already touched on, and we will have a lot more to say about it in Chapter 6. Strides have been made in improving the validity of the interview, and it is no longer the pariah it was among academics but, with the best will in the world, it cannot be classed as a high validity method for selecting good people. It is fine to use it for the purpose of discussion between employer and possible employee, the decision to make an offer having already been made. Then it does no harm. But to use it as a cutting edge to try to find the very best candidates is not supported, given all that we know. Can it be put any earlier in the process as a blunt tool to do some screening? Possibly so, but being labour-intensive it is bound to be costly. Having said that, one organization we know does hold a first interview, and places it at stage two of the process, using it to knock out applicants, with a second interview at the very end. That second interview does, however, very much count.

PLANNING THE PROCESS

Undoubtedly, planning a recruitment and selection process is calculated to give you a headache. This is because there are so many variables to consider. These are summarised in Box 3.2.

Mapping out your overall process on the basis of these variables can be a relatively smooth affair – if you are only using one selection method.

BOX 3.2   VARIABLES TO CONSIDER WHEN DESIGNING A PROCESS

The variables commonly considered at this point are:

- number of vacancies
- likely number of applications
- likely selection ratio (number of candidates to number of vacancies)
- validity of available methods
- time available
- budget/resources
- expertise (assessment centre design, level A and B qualifications).

Psychologists have constructed 'expectancy tables' which can tell you whether the costs associated with any particular method are justified on the basis of the number of people you are likely to recruit[7]. When you are planning a sequenced recruitment process, the calculations are much more complex. Rather than get in to such complexities, we provide a simple checklist – Table 3.2 – which can be used as a decision tool when trying to plan a sequence of selection methods.

	Application form	Tests	Personality question-naires	Work samples	Interviews	Assessment centres
Cost	L	M	M	M	M	H
Validity	M	H	M	H	H	H
High vs low volume	H	H	L	H	L	L
Coarse vs* fine grain	L	L	M	M	M	H
Best position	Front	Middle	End	Mid-end	Mid-end	End

*Fine grain instruments are 'sharp' tools capable of distinguishing between similar candidates. Coarse grain instruments are 'blunt' tools more useful for bulk sifting.
Key: H = High (or fine grain); M = Medium; L = Low (or coarse grain)

Table 3.2   A Decision Tool for Planning a Sequenced Recruitment Process

WHAT ACTUALLY HAPPENS IN PRACTICE?

We have talked about ways of planning the whole process, what the constituent parts should be, and what order they should come in, but what is actually going on out there? For some insights, we are indebted to a recent survey – the EDB survey[8] – which we shall make reference to throughout the book.

The most significant influence in the choice of selection methods for any one vacancy is the type of job. Typically, employers seeking to fill clerical/secretarial vacancies use *three* different methods to select new recruits. The most important is usually the interview, which is often conducted in a single stage with two interviewers. Of secondary importance are application forms and ability tests.

Graduates can also be expected to be exposed to three different selection methods when applying for jobs. Interviews are universal and application forms very common for this group. The most important parts of the selection process tend to be the interview stage (commonly two interviews, each with two interviewers) and the application form – although employers who use assessment centres find them to be a very useful part of the process. A forthcoming survey by colleagues will shed further light on what is really happening out there for graduates.

Selection processes for managers are reported to be the most complicated of all. Most commonly, four different methods are used, the most important of which (as with all job types) is the interview, with at least two interview stages attended by three or more interviewers. Managers are also likely to be asked to take some kind of formal test, either an ability test or a personality questionnaire, or both.

Manual/craft employees face the least arduous selection processes. Usually they can expect to undergo just two or three selection methods, most commonly the application form and/or CV and a single interview with two interviewers. As for professional/technical staff, they can expect to go through roughly what the graduate receives with the exception that assessment centres are far less often used on this group.

The relative take up of the various methods is summarized in Figure 3.2*.

Whether it is an en bloc or a sequenced process, the object of the exercise is to assess applicants on the competencies identified as important to successful performance in the job. Thus, competencies have to be married to methods. How this might work is shown in Table 3.3 for Fettercorn's selection and recruitment process.

---

* Reproduced by kind permission of IRS

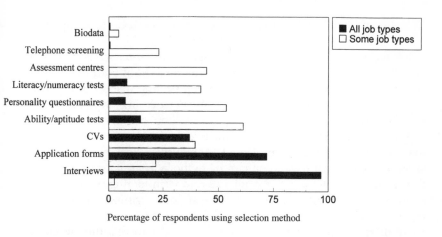

Percentage of respondents using selection method

Figure 3.2　Selection Methods used by Employers

Competencies	Stage I Application form	Stage II First interview	Work sample tests	Stage III Assessment centre
Analysis	✓		✓	✓
Learning ability	✓		✓	✓
Influencing	✓	✓		✓
Interpersonal skills	✓	✓		✓
Achievement drive	✓	✓		✓
Planning and organizing	✓	✓		✓

Table 3.3　The Three Stages of Fettercorn's Recruitment and Selection Process

Stage I – Application form

The first element of the process is the application form. In the case of Fettercorn, it taps into all of the competencies, but this may not always be necessary. Much will depend on what the job analysis has thrown up. If there are four competencies which emerge as 'must haves', it may be sensible to use only these on the application form, or to place them first on the form and discard applicants as soon as they 'fail'. In terms of sifting time, there should be a trade-off; an application form with six competencies will take longer to sift, but you should receive less of them, as only the extremely keen applicants will take the time to complete the entire form (we say more on this in Chapter 5).

It is worth bearing in mind that the application form itself is informative about your organization, and therefore can be used in your favour. If the competencies included in the application form have names like 'Controlling others', 'Coping with stress', or 'Persevering indefinitely', the applicant will get a certain impression. It will not be the same impression as that gained from a form which includes competencies such as 'Tolerance for others', 'Team work', and 'Achievement drive'. Not that this should be used as a reason for sanitizing the labels put on competencies, but language matters, and if you can avoid intimidating or authoritarian sounding names, then do so. Of course, if your organization is all about command and control, and working all hours, then be true to yourself and leave those competencies as they are. You will find that they work very well as a *realistic job preview* in turning off possible unsuitable applicants (see Chapter 4).

Stage II – First interview and work sample tests

Fettercorn's stage two consists of a short screening interview targeting four competencies already identified as crucial, and two bespoke work samples which tap into 'Learning ability' and 'Analytical'.

The choice of competencies to assess in the interview will depend (obviously) on which competencies actually lend themselves to being assessed in the interview. For example, it makes little sense to assess 'Analysis' in a face-to-face interview. It is better done by a test or exercise. However, 'Influencing' is an obvious choice for an interview.

Then there is the overall coverage of competencies. A good rule of thumb is that all competencies need to be assessed at least twice during the process, although, of course, that will not apply to the weaker applicants who are discarded early.

Stage III – Assessment centre

The assessment centre covers all six competencies. What is more, within the assessment centre each competency will be measured at least twice. For Fettercorn, there is a second interview which is part of the assessment centre. But it also serves another important function, which is the one of information exchange we talked about earlier. Preferred candidates should be encouraged to ask questions, 'Where is Fettercorn going?', 'What development will I get?', 'Who will I be working with?', 'How are bonuses decided?', and so on, and receive the kind of answers which will enable them to decide whether they want to work for the company. We describe the Fettercorn assessment centre more fully in Chapter 9.

SUMMARY

Although there is a tendency for people – professionals and researchers – to focus on individual elements in the recruitment and selection process (the interviews, tests, etc.), we have tried to encourage a view of the process 'in the round'. A consideration of which methods best measure which competencies at which point – which are best suited to high volumes of applicants and which are the best at making fine distinctions between high-grade candidates – should help organisations construct a process most suited to their needs, and with high overall utility.

FETTERCORN plc – A CASE STUDY

One week later, Jack was back in Ros's office. It had been a long day, but they had finally thrashed out a blueprint recruitment and selection process for the Head Buyer role. Based on Ros's budget, and the information Jack had provided about the various selection methods (and how they might fit together), they had finally agreed on the following:

Numbers	Stage	Method
$N = 600$		Recruitment advertisement
$N = 200$	I	CV (for technical screening) and competency-based application form
$N = 30$	II	Competency-based screening interview, work sample tests
$N = 8$	III	Assessment centre

The numbers were guesstimates, but having some ball-park figures would at least give Ros a baseline for decision making if the number of replies to the advert greatly exceeded or fell short of the target.

'That was a good day's work,' said Ros. 'Just before you go, I need some help with this whole business of how we attract applicants. You don't have to rush off, do you?'

REFERENCES

1. Latham, G.P. and Whyte, G. (1994). The futility of utility analysis. *Personnel Psychology*, **47** (1), 31–47.
2. Goffin, R.D., Rothstein, M.G. and Johnston, N.G. (1996). Personality testing and the assessment center: Incremental validity for managerial selection. *Journal of Applied Psychology*, **81** (6), 746–756.
3. Robertson, I.T. and Downs, S. (1989). Work sample tests of trainability: a meta-analysis. *Journal of Applied Psychology*, **74**, 402–410.
   Schmitt, N.B., Goodwin, R.Z., Noe, R.A. and Krisch, M. (1984). Meta analysis of validity studies published between 1964 and 1982 and the investigation of study characteristics. *Personnel Psychology*, **37**, 407–422.
4. Wood, R., Hamer, G., Johnson, C.E. and Payne, T. (1997). Selecting for a profession: A case study. In Anderson, N.R. and Herriot, P. (Eds) *International Handbook of Selection and Assessment*. Chichester: Wiley, 1997.
5. Payne, T.J., Anderson, N.R. and Smith, T. (1992). Assessment centres, selection systems and cost-effectiveness, *Personnel Review*, **21**, 48–56.
6. Ruderman, M. and Ohlott, P.J. (1990). *Traps and Pitfalls in the Judgement of Executive Potential*. Greensboro, NC: Center For Creative Leadership.
7. Smith, M. and Robertson, I.T. (1993). *The Theory and Practice of Systematic Personnel Selection (2nd Edition)*. London: Macmillan.
8. Employee Development Bulletin (1997). The state of selection: An IRS survey. *EDB 85*.

Attracting the right applicants (but not too many)* **4**

Our purpose in this chapter is to examine the bothersome problem – because that is what it is – of attracting applicants; not just any applicants but the right applicants. We discuss the difficulties faced by the well known high profile organizations, and by the less well known employers. We identify the importance of managing the applicant pool, and describe three steps to doing this effectively – sending a clear message, understanding your applicants, and sifting out the unwanted. We identify two alternative approaches to sending a clear message, using values and using competencies, and conclude with a discussion of recruitment advertising.

FETTERCORN plc – A CASE STUDY

'Organizations usually fall into one of two categories,' said Jack. 'The ones that receive too many applications, from both appropriate and inappropriate applicants, and the ones that do not receive enough applications.' He went on, 'This is usually determined by your organization's image – high profile companies like Virgin, just to name one, tend to attract large postbags, whilst lower profile organizations – particularly those in the public sector – are liable to receive less interest.'

'Interesting,' said Ros. 'I guess that although we don't have a strong public image, and indeed have difficulty recruiting graduates,

---

* Part of this chapter is based on an article previously published by CCH Editions Ltd: Payne, T. (1997). How to attract the right job applicants. *Personnel Management Newsletter*, 3, pp. 2–5.

we are well known for our state-of-the-art buying department, particularly within the buying community. I don't think we should have too
much trouble attracting enough candidates.'

'In that case,' said Jack, 'you have a different problem: how to
make sure only the better candidates apply. You need to target the
high flyers quite precisely, and persuade those who might otherwise
apply "on spec" to screen themselves out. Too many applicants,
and someone is going to have to give up their weekend for some
intensive sifting activity.'

Although not convinced that 'intensive sifting activity' was a bona
fide term and not consultant-speak, Ros saw the logic in what Jack
was saying. This was clearly a critical stage, and she needed to be
sure to get it right. 'So what are our options?'

In 1996, tired of recruiting through the usual channels, and wanting to
recruit graduates to train as store managers, Asda placed an advert in *Viz*.
Featuring a picture of a giant jelly, it read: 'At Asda we have plenty of jelly,
but no moulds.' The gamble, if it was that, paid off. Asda received nearly
200 responses to the advert and three applicants were eventually hired. An
Asda personnel spokesman remarked, 'The adverts in the *Guardian* are
much of a type and we thought maybe we could look at different types of
store managers – ones with a sense of humour.'[1]

It doesn't matter what you think of *Viz*, or *ID*, where Asda have also
advertised – the point is the importance of, first, attraction and then
mutual attraction. Here is something employers will need to pay increasing attention to, especially when recruiting graduates. The number of
graduates coming out of the universities is increasing faster than the
number of graduate entry-level jobs. This will inevitably lead to higher
numbers of applications, larger and less appropriate applicant pools, and
increasing problems in managing and sifting these applicant pools.

Even so, there will continue to be 'hot spots' where applicants with
certain skills will enjoy a seller's market. Often cited examples are city
traders and IT specialists. In these situations, the traditional selection
practices which focus on the organisation ('who should we choose?') need
to change to practices more centred on the individual ('how can we get
those we want to accept our offers?'). It therefore becomes necessary to
think about what future employees might want. While it seems unlikely to
apply to traders, there is research[2] which shows salary to be some way
down the list of students' 'must haves'. The consistent top three are: type
of work, the kind of people you would like to work with, and training and
development opportunities.

MANAGING YOUR APPLICANT POOL

Many, perhaps most, organizations have difficulty in attracting the right applicants. By 'right', we mean the right *number* of applicants, with the right *level* of basic ability, aptitude and overall 'potential', and the right *attitude* to the organisation. The ideal outcome of a recruitment campaign is a small number of high potential applicants who are committed to the organisation, its values, and its core business. This, as any recruitment professional will tell you, is extremely difficult to achieve. For example:

- Organizations with a high public profile, such as Marks & Spencer and British Airways receive huge amounts of applications. Many are from people who know few specific facts about the company or what it stands for, but whose perception seems to be informed by vague notions such as, 'it has a good reputation, therefore it must be a good place to work,' or, perhaps, in the case of British Airways, 'I fancy all that free travel' (not true).

- Organizations with low public profiles – and many in the public sector fall into this category – often receive much smaller numbers of applications. Whilst this is cheaper and more convenient to manage, these organizations run the risk of missing out on the diversity of talent available to them. All the sophistication in the world will not help you select a high flyer if none apply to you for a job.

- Some sectors, and indeed some organizations, find it difficult to attract ethnic minority applicants. There is the retail sector, for example, which in any case has great difficulty attracting the best young people, for whom the poor image is a turnoff[3]. Perhaps it is part of the greater recruitment problem but the evidence suggests that despite making great efforts in this area, this sector receives fewer applications from ethnic minorities than would be expected from their numbers. Again, organizations with this problem have a reduced diversity of talent from which to select.

Organizations must learn to manage their applicant pools. This can only happen when the communication between you and your potential applicants is clear, two-way, and meaningful. In order to successfully manage applicant pools, you will need to concentrate on:

- sending a clear message
- understanding your applicants
- putting off the unsuited.

Sending a clear message

To help organizations and individuals find each other, you must make it absolutely clear to potential applicants what it is your organisation stands for, what the core identity is which will not be compromised; where your individuality and distinctiveness lie. For example, if you are a merchant bank which places a premium on creativity and innovation, make that clear in all your dealings with potential applicants, through your advertising, your recruitment brochure if you have one, and your selection process. Narrowing down the applicant pool on this basis we feel should ensure a diverse yet manageable pool of applicants from which to select the most suitable recruits. We see two alternative approaches here – values-based recruitment and competency-based recruitment.

Values *vs* competencies – alternative or complementary?

To evaluate the two options, we need to touch on the relationship between values and their more visible cousins, competencies. The relationship hinges on diversity; that is, taking advantage of it. As we noted before, Binna Kandola has argued[4] that recruiting against competencies could in theory lead to an organization full of clones, which in turn could lead to a failure to get out of the box and, in the extreme, to collapse. Indeed, he argues that the only reason this does not occur is that our selection methods are not completely accurate.

The cloning argument needs some qualification. It appears to us that employers want from employees the same three things – to have a good mind, get on with people, and be organized and keen (thinking, feeling and acting, again). It is how the three are expressed in the individual that is interesting, and this is the point at which values come in. Because people with the same values will not necessarily have the same personalities or working styles, using values as decision making criteria ought to remove any dangers of cloning.

Perhaps values could replace competencies completely (with perhaps some measure of ability included), or perhaps they should be used to complement a more traditional competency-based procedure. Let us consider values first.

Values-based recruitment – identifying and communicating your values

Here is a statement about core values:

> Companies that enjoy enduring success have core
> values and a core purpose that remain fixed while their
> business strategies and practices endlessly adapt to a
> changing world[5].

Core values, say these authors, are the 'essential and enduring tenets of an
organization. A small set of timeless guiding principles ... core values
have intrinsic value to those inside the organisation'. Core values, when
truly internalised and realised, say an awful lot about an organisation –
perhaps they tell you all you need to know. Consider the examples that
Collins and Porras cite:

Walt Disney:

- no cynicism
- nurturing and promulgation of 'wholesome American values'
- creativity, dreams and imagination
- fanatical attention to consistency and detail
- preservation and control of the Disney magic.

Philip Morris:

- the right to freedom of choice
- winning – beating others in a good fight
- encouraging individual initiative
- opportunity based on merit; no one is entitled to anything
- hard work and continuous self-improvement.

Sony:

- elevation of the Japanese culture and national status
- being a pioneer – not following others; doing the impossible
- encouraging individual ability and creativity.

Nordstrom:

- service to the customer above all else
- hard work and individual productivity

- never being satisfied
- excellence in reputation; being part of something special.

These short simple statements give more of a flavour of what it would be like to work in these companies than any number of 'personal testimonies' or case studies. The most impressive thing about them is their honesty – they certainly would not appeal to all. For example, we doubt whether the person who is attracted to apply to Philip Morris ('winning', 'beating others in a good fight') would also be tempted to apply to Walt Disney ('no cynicism', 'nurturing and promulgation of "wholesome American values" ').

One of the key challenges for recruiters is to persuade applicants (particularly graduates) to put the effort into differentiating between employers and between positions, and to target their applications. After all, looking at it from their point of view it may make sense to use the scattergun approach; the more applications they send, the greater the likelihood of getting an interview, and ultimately a job. That said, forcing people, in the nicest possible way, to think about who they are applying to, and why, must surely make the recruitment process more efficient for both parties.

Competency-based recruitment – identifying and communicating your competencies

There is no doubt; the line between competencies and values is a thin one. As we discussed in Chapter 2, the modern competency framework may contain a mish-mash of 'true' competencies, psychological characteristics, business imperatives, and even values. Is not the organization which includes 'customer service' as a key selection criteria saying something about its core values? Just as Nordstrom in the example above labelled 'service to the customer above all else' a value (Nordstrom is a department store), so we know many organizations who would label the same statement a competency.

Using competencies as a way of communicating clearly with your applicant pool is a good idea, and in many settings works well. We go on to describe some proper competency-based adverts at the end of the chapter. What we are becoming somewhat wary of is the use of competencies as a communication tool during graduate recruitment. The difficulty is that at this level, many competency frameworks are similar (see Box 4.1).

In the end it comes back to the position we set out at the beginning of this book. The true value of a competency-based approach to human resource deployment lies in its integrating function. Because of this, we still think that using competencies as a means to communicate with applicants is the best way for many organizations – particularly large organizations that have integrated competencies through the HR system. For smaller organizations, like ourselves, we suspect values-based recruitment offers a more imaginative and ultimately more effective approach.

BOX 4.1 COMPETENCIES, APPLICATION FORMS AND GRADUATE RECRUITMENT

Most large organizations ultimately want the same graduate raw material to work with – skills in analyzing, making things happen, and dealing with people (perhaps with some business awareness thrown in). The difficulty comes when organizations try to use competencies to differentiate themselves in the marketplace, as often the competencies are similar. The competencies from three current graduate application forms are shown below:

Coopers & Lybrand	ICL	BA
Drive and initiative	Initiative	Leadership
Interpersonal skills	Getting ideas across	Communication
Problem solving	Problem solving	Problem analysis
Commitment to a		Team working
business career		Learning orientation
		Innovation/risk

Understanding your applicants

The second step to managing your applicant pool is to understand that applicant pool. Even a group as apparently homogenous as graduates varies in its value systems, interests, motives and needs. Different people value different things. Studies in this area have presented lists of organizational characteristics to people and asked them to put them in order of importance. The results turn out to be remarkably consistent. We have already remarked on the top three. Here is the full list which emerged from research with students[6]:

- Type of work you would do

- Type of people you would like to work with
- Training and development opportunities
- Chances of promotion
- Salary
- Job security
- Working conditions
- Reputation/image of organization
- Geographical location
- Hours expected to work
- Benefits (company car, pension, etc.)

It is likely that the order of this list will change as people grow and develop. Once a family arrives, hours, security and location are likely to assume more importance. When entering the third age, benefits may become more attractive. This, and other factors, limit the value of this approach. We have since taken a different approach in our research; that is to ask people to rate a list of adjectives used to describe organizations in terms of how important these characteristics would be when deciding who to apply to. When we did this, we found more variation. Indeed, in the first phase of this research concentrating on students, we identified four 'big' constructs which students in our sample used when weighing up organizations[7]. These are shown in Table 4.1.

The same methodology can be used with other homogenous applicant groups to identify how an organization is seen in relation to adjectival descriptors. An example is shown in Figure 4.1.

The power of this approach (which utilizes the statistical technique called multidimensional scaling) is that it pinpoints or encapsulates how organizations are perceived. For example, in Figure 4.1, we can see that organization 'X' is associated with the adjectives 'small', 'community-based' and 'local', and not at all with 'professional', 'fun', 'financially secure', or 'demanding'. If there is a mismatch between reality and perceived image, the organization knows it has work to do.

Another advantage of this sort of research is that organizations can learn how to present their recruitment message in language which is meaningful to potential applicants. 'Personal contribution' is a competency we have come across. Is it meaningful to applicants? Probably not, but words like 'respectful', 'loyal' and 'dependable' will be.

There is, of course, a danger in this approach. Experience shows that job seekers are quite a cynical lot, and are quick to identify any contradiction between espoused values and actual practice. Reaction to the publicity the

Maternal	Bottom-line	Professional	Exciting
Loyal	High profile	Respectful	Stimulating
Safe	Profit-driven	Ethical	Risky
Family-friendly	Cut throat	Professional	Fun
Protective	(Ethical)	Values-driven	Creative
Community-based	Large	High-tech	Adventurous
Dependable	Demanding	Efficient	Enthusiastic
Caring	(Green)	Diverse	International
Respectful	Financially secure	Fair	
Local			
Trusting			
Friendly			
Equal opportunities			
Nurturing			
Socially conscious			

(N.B Adjectives in brackets load negatively onto the factor)

Table 4.1   Constructs Students use to Weigh up Organizations

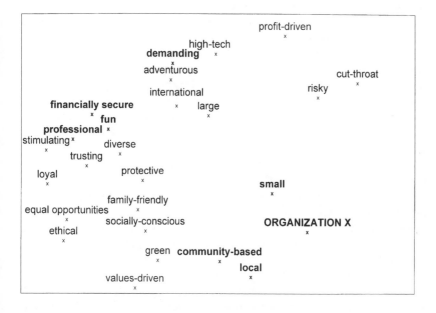

Figure 4.1   How Undergraduates see Organization 'X'

Ford motor company received in relation to their equal opportunities practice (painting out black faces in adverts) was extremely negative. Any perceived mismatch between image and practice is likely to create a negative impact.

Putting off the unsuited

It is important to communicate what the job will actually entail, warts and all. This is sometimes called a *realistic job preview* (RJP). The RJP works on the principle that if people are told enough about the job, and are able to assess themselves and their prospects realistically and unsentimentally, then they should be able to screen themselves in or out. The importance of the job preview cannot be underestimated: it gets the numbers down and it cuts the costs of recruitment.

Job previews may be of the *enhancement* type, designed to enhance overly pessimistic expectations, or the *reduction* type, designed to reduce overly optimistic expectations. There is research[8] which indicates that RJPs can be successful in doing what they are supposed to do, especially the reduction type, and it is reduction generally that is wanted. However, it is possible to err too much in the other direction. When recruiting occupational psychologists for our own organization, a self-assessment questionnaire, which itself functions as an RJP, has proved to be useful because the questions serve to convey not only the nature of the job but also what we expect from the people we employ. Usually, we have no trouble attracting applicants but on one particular occasion the returns were very thin indeed. After a prolonged inquest, it was concluded that the requirement for 'selling' experience had been over-emphasized and that this had frightened off a lot of possible applicants. Our psychologists need to be able to sell but not to the extent that was perhaps communicated.

Just having to fill in an application form can persuade some people to opt out. Knowledge of what the process as a whole entails can have the same effect. An example occurred in the second year of the Inns of Court School of Law selection process (see Chapter 3). Year 1 of the process had been relatively easy, with only a critical reasoning test to be taken. In year 2, however, the process became seriously challenging. Now there was an oral test to be undergone, and three written tests, also a structured application form. This was altogether more daunting. It was no great surprise to us when the applicant numbers fell one third from 2200 to 1500. Those who applied knew what they were letting themselves in for (we have to presume) and (we also presume) those who did not fancy going through the process selected themselves out.

Apart from through the application form, RJPs can be communicated through a job description, through a brochure, through material specially developed for inclusion in an application pack, through an interview, provided the applicant thinks to ask, and through the advertisement (not to mention the best type of RJP – work experience). But it may still not be enough to discourage those who are still intent on using the scatter-gun approach to finding a job. The key here is to require applicants to *make an effort* and actually do some work over and above that needed to fill out the application form and read the brochure. Examples of how this can be made to happen are:

- researching the organization
- self-assessment questionnaires
- work experience requirement.

ADVERTISEMENTS

The advertisement is the place where the organization makes its bid to attract the applicants it wants. The two crucial factors are content and placement. What you say and where you say it will have a determining effect on the quality and quantity of applications you receive. If you put the ad where most people put theirs there will be a trade-off between exposure and genuine engagement. You are assured of a large audience but not of their undivided attention. In these circumstances, the RJP is unlikely to function as intended, and is therefore a waste of effort. While the *Guardian* is the place for a large audience (according to a recent survey[9] it holds the lead in the national newspaper advertising market with a 37 per cent market share), some organizations are becoming more adventurous in where they place ads, as we saw from the *Viz* example.

Wherever the advert is placed, the wording is absolutely vital (and one decision may affect the other). That is true whether the ad is going to be phrased in competency or values language. Here is an advertisement which is very definitely *not* phrased in competency (or values) language.

> *A rare opportunity for an outgoing PA to join this presti- gious PR Consultancy based in Mayfair. Using your excellent secretarial skills 80/60 you will provide support to two dynamic and charming individuals. The role will involve plenty of contact with well-known clients, research- ing and organizing presentations. You should be a confident communicator with a warm personality who would enjoy being part of this busy and exciting environment.*

Because it is written in such loose but grabby language – 'dynamic and charming', 'warm personality' – this advertisement is almost certain to bring in far too many of the wrong applicants. What, apart from the speed requirement, is there to turn people off, or make them think? It's glamorous, and it helps to be a luvvy, darling. Oh, and a secretary when you can manage it.

Here is another ad for a PA. Compared to the last, it is much more sober and structured; in fact, with its mix of generic and technical competencies, it begins to approximate to what a competency-based advertisement would look like. Here is part of the advertisement:

> **Key requirements are:**
> *Excellent administrative, organizational and secretarial skills*
> *Strong communication skills at a senior level*
> *Fast and accurate typing*
> *Proficiency in the use of Microsoft Office*
> *Applicants should have a confident and mature manner.*

There is enough in this advertisement to enable people to screen themselves out. Sometimes the desire to attract via a strong, individual message conflicts with offering a realistic job preview, or itemizing the competencies required. Another Asda advert, 'George', this time for its clothing division, trades entirely on the pulling power of George Davies, the ex-Next maestro. After introducing George, all the ad says is, 'So if you want to be trained in fashion and business by one of the best, we have a development programme ... .'[10]Let's hope they got what they wanted from what must have been a massive sift, especially as the ad was headed 'Dynamic Graduates'.

Here, however, is an advert with an impeccable RJP. Nobody, but nobody, would put in for this job unless they met the requirements ... and what requirements they are.

> *We are seeking a Rosewood Furniture Repair Master in our London branch who shall be able to repair and touch up rosewood furniture; carry out quality control of imported furniture; stock control; liaise with factories; carry our consumer surveys; and carry out on site service and repair furniture.*
>
> *The candidate should have a minimum of 6 years experience in a related field, be able to speak English, Mandarin and Cantonese, be familiar with Chinese Arts and Crafts and*

> *must have experience in classical rosewood furniture and previous exhibitions organization skill (sic).*

Asda may have felt that competency talk was less than sexy, somewhat earnest bordering on the dull, and we could relate to that. But you have to ask where glam-talk gets you. Search and selection agencies sooner or later cannot resist the temptation of piling on the hyperbole and generally going over the top. In one example of the genre, what started out as a reasonably focused advert more or less couched in competency language – strong intellect, negotiation skills, business awareness – becomes this:

> *Vigorous and inspirational leader, strong on implementation and change management. Results driven with sharp commercial instincts and the ability to work through people developing cross cultural affinity whilst generating a positive impact on service delivery and financial performance.*

At least some restraint was shown: 'charismatic', so beloved of headhunters, is replaced by 'inspirational'.

Here is another one: it is not just communication skills that are wanted but *consummate* communication skills, whatever those are. In addition, the appointee has not only to be 'consistently detail-conscious' and 'accurate in situations where there is no room for error' but also 'innovative' and 'solution-orientated'. Richard Branson might just qualify on most of this (if he had not blotted his copybook with his last balloon trip); in fact, you may be amazed to learn, a company secretary is wanted. In our experience, attention to detail and big picture thinking are seldom found in the same person, which does not mean that those who cannot do one can do the other (cf. our remarks on compensatory mind sets in Chapter 2).

Sober they may be, but some of the best ads manage to convey the distinctiveness of the organization while at the same time making it perfectly clear what the job is, and who should apply. The latter is often accomplished by including what amounts to a job specification and a personal specification, set side by side in bullet point format and headed respectively, 'The job' and 'You'.

SUMMARY

In the opening chapter we predicted that attraction of appropriate numbers of suitable applicants will increasingly become a hot topic. In this chapter we have set out three key steps to successfully managing your applicant pool: sending a clear message (where we considered both values-based and competency-based communication), understanding your applicants, and putting off unsuitable potential applicants. We concluded with a discussion of competency-based advertisements, illustrating how they can function as effective realistic job previews. In the next chapter we move on to look in more detail at the application process in practice.

FETTERCORN plc – A CASE STUDY

So much for the weekend saved from so called 'intensive sifting activity' – Ros eventually spent it getting her advertisement right. She decided to put it into a quality broadsheet, specifically into the executive recruitment supplement. As the job would have specialist appeal only, that seemed appropriate. The ad could not be too large (she was on a budget) but it had to make an impact. She thought of *Viz*, but rejected it. If she found a Head Buyer with a sense of humour, that would be a bonus.

Later, on the 'phone to Jack, she brought him up to date. 'The ad is structured around the six competencies, of course, and there is also to be some RJP material concentrated on the biggest challenge of all for the job-holder – influencing in the context of negotiation. 'I know you were dubious about it but it is true – 1 per cent saved by a buyer can mean 15 per cent on gross profits!'

'I believe you,' said Jack. 'Fax it over, and I'll have a final look.' 'Too late I'm afraid,' laughed Ros, 'it's already gone. Don't worry though, I'm sure after all of your expensive advice, it will be just fine.'

Here is Ros's ad as it appeared.

FETTERCORN plc

Head Buyer (circa £45K + performance-related bonus and generous benefits package)

A leading purveyor of exclusive gourmet foodstuffs currently embarked on global expansion wishes to appoint a Head Buyer to deal with the implications of growth in the international supply chain.

Key requirements for the job are shown below.

Can you . . .

- analyse global performance data and make decisions?
- learn from your mistakes and the mistakes of others?
- influence people and negotiate a competitive deal?
- communicate clearly with a wide range of people?
- plan for and organize a team of buyers?
- achieve results when under pressure?

If you can answer these questions, and can back this up with evidence at interview, then please telephone Ros Fairburn, Human Resource Manager Fettercorn plc on 01865 772299 or write to her at Human Resource Department, 353 Maxwell Road, Botley, Oxford, OX3 5ZT for an application form. You will be asked to submit a CV with the application form. Closing date is January 31st.

REFERENCES

1. Teather, D. (1996). Think outside the box. *Recruitment Today*, October, 16–17.
2. Based on research by Whiddett and Payne (1994), and Keane, Kandola and Payne (1996). Both in-house research reports for Pearn Kandola.
3. Kimber, A. (1996). Shopping around. *Recruitment Today*, October, 21–22.
4. Kandola, R.S. (1996). Putting competencies in perspective. *Competency*, **4** (1), 31–34.
5. Collins, J.C. and Porras, J.I. (1996). Building your company's vision. *Harvard Business Review*, September–October.
6. Whiddett, S., Payne, T. and Kandola, R. (1995). Organizational preferences: are public and private sector organizations perceived differently as potential employers? *Occupational Psychology Conference Book of Proceedings*, 205–211.
7. Payne, T. (1997). How to attract the right job applicants. *Personnel management newsletter*, **3**, 2–5.
8. Meglino, B.M. *et al* (1988). Effects of realistic job previews: A comparison using an enhancement and a reduction preview. *Journal of Applied Psychology*, **73**, 259–266.
   Wanous, J.P. (1989). Installing a realistic job: Ten tough options. *Personnel Psychology*, **42**, 117–134.
9. *Recruitment Today*, October 1996, Yardstick Feature (back page).
10. Teather, D. (1996). Think outside the box. *Recruitment Today*, October 16–17.

Application Form Design and Sifting 5

In this chapter, we discuss ways of handling large numbers of application forms. We consider the purpose and design of application forms, specifically competency-based forms, biodata forms and CVs. We describe the immediate discard method of sifting, and point out how equal opportunities can be jeopardized.

FETTERCORN plc – A CASE STUDY

The ad Ros placed brought many requests for an application form. She and Jack had spent a couple of days designing and trialling the form on the current buying team, and they were confident that it would do the job. The information it requested was directly tied to the competencies needed to do the job and, not only that, it would provide a clear platform for the competency-based structured interview which the successful candidates would face later in the process.

Ros looked at the clock in her office. It was six o'clock on a Friday night, and she could murder a pint of Guinness, but she had a few things to finish up first. She had a review of progress with Jack on Monday, and she wanted to find a way to shave a few hundred pounds off his bill, or at least make him sweat a little.

'Mind you,' she thought, 'I learned some valuable lessons about application forms in the last few weeks.' As part of the design process, the two of them had reviewed the available literature, critiqued the forms used by other companies, and Ros had picked Jack's brain for his experience with his other clients.

'I think some of these learning points are too good to lose,' thought Ros. Putting the Guinness on hold for another 30 minutes, she began to type up her experiences . . .

THE APPLICATIONS AVALANCHE AND HOW TO COPE

In an average year across the police service, there are some 60 to 80,000 applications for 5 to 6000 positions as probationer constable. Merely to process the applications causes logistical problems. Other public services, like the fire service, are similarly inundated, as are those employers to whom graduates are especially fond of applying, like British Airways, Marks and Spencer, and so on. In one graduate recruitment drive for marketing and general management training, 2365 applications were received, 18 were made offers, and 15 (0.76 per cent of applications!) accepted.

The challenge facing human resource professionals, particularly when faced with numbers like these, is how to reduce the applications to a more manageable number in a way which is reliable, valid, fair and, just as important, cost effective. The process of reducing numbers of applications is known as sifting (or sometimes screening). The keys to effective sifting are:

- design of the application form

- construction of a marking scheme

- willingness to wield the axe.

In the drive just mentioned, 92 per cent of applicants were rejected on the strength of their application form, so that only (only?) 183 went to preliminary interview. To enable an efficient sift of this many application forms, it is vital that the sifter knows what information he or she is looking for, and can get at it easily. This is why the *design of the form* is so important. Imagine trying to sift more than two thousand application forms with only the vague hope that 'I'll know it when I see it' to sustain you!

The sift is speeded enormously if there is a *marking scheme,* or set of decision rules to permit quick decisions about applications. If the form is properly structured, and the numbers are high, it should be possible to reject applicants as soon as they fail a hurdle, and before marking of the form is complete. Thus as soon as an applicant fails a section, that person is deemed to be rejected. This we call the *immediate discard technique,* and it can save much time and money. More generally, the discard rule is unlikely to be as severe as this; it would more likely be framed along these lines, 'Reject if marks on two of the five sections do not exceed the pass mark'. But how severe you make it depends entirely on the ratio of applicants to jobs available – for the police it is of the order of 15 to 1. We shall discuss the immediate discard technique in more detail later. Above all else though, it is important to be consistent in the criteria that you are applying. Failure to do this will compromise the utility of the system at the point where you have the widest diversity of talent to choose from.

It may seem odd to be talking about 'marking' an application form, as if it were a test, but that is precisely what it is. The knack is to get it performing like one. That involves introducing structure and objectivity as a means of getting strong behavioural evidence. For it to work effectively, however, you have to be prepared to *wield the axe*. You need to trust your process and have confidence in applying the rules. Do not get into the habit of parking applicants, or putting them on hold – 'if in doubt, knock it out'.

THE APPLICATION FORM: SECOND MOST INFLUENTIAL SELECTION TOOL

According to the EDB survey[1], the application form is seen as the *second most influential* tool in the selection process after the interview. The proportion rating it as among the top three methods for selection ranged from 35.7 per cent for managerial posts to 58.6 per cent for manual/craft jobs. The CV, which is of course a free-form application form where the applicant decides the format, was, interestingly, rated as the third most important selection method. It was, and is, particularly favoured by finance houses (although that should be tempered by the fact that they made relatively heavy use of almost all of the nine selection methods covered by the survey).

All in all, the EDB survey indicates that application forms or CVs tend to be the second factor influencing selection decisions after the impact of the interview has been considered. Actually, the power of the application form is potentially even greater than that, given that it is used to screen out such large numbers of applicants (see Chapter 3).

The current state of affairs

A recent survey[2] of 536 high-volume recruiters produced some frightening statistics about the use of application forms. Ninety-four (94) per cent of respondents indicated that application forms were used to screen out applicants. Organizations varied in the proportion of applicants that were rejected using this method. At one extreme, 30 per cent of organizations screened out less than one in three. At the other, 15 per cent rejected more than seven out of ten applicants. This is clearly a high proportion – one would have to be very confident of the validity of the application form as a screen, and of the skill of the people doing the sifting. However, and this is the most scary fact, 82 per cent of organizations failed to provide *any* guidelines for the screeners on how to interpret the information in the application form, and only just over half of the organizations provided any formal training to those people. Not only that, but those screening out higher proportions of applicants were less likely to provide guidelines or training, and in a third of cases the screen was carried out by only one person. Finally, only half the organizations reported using a specially designed application form, and of these, only 14 had conducted any kind of pilot study.

These results are particularly distressing. At the point in the recruitment process where the most candidates are rejected, organizations are using either off the shelf or untested application forms, and asking people with no training to make significant decisions. The damage that this could do to your chances of landing the best recruits is clear.

What happens when sifters are left to their own devices?

What little research evidence there is paints a bleak picture. One study[3] asked those making the decisions to think aloud whilst making them. Sifters tended to make assumptions about personality, motivation and job knowledge from the information they were given, rather than use the information itself. They also gave significantly more weight to negative information (a finding which also holds true for other selection methods, including interviews and references). In other words, rather than look for evidence for specific criteria (such as competencies), they make general judgements (or halos), with all of the problems which that entails.

In the remainder of this chapter, we shall consider three ways of structuring applications:

- competency-based application forms

- biodata

- CVs.

COMPETENCY-BASED APPLICATION FORMS

The competency-based application form requires applicants to provide evidence, which means examples from their experience, that they will be able to demonstrate the competency when required. The response format is written, usually 100 words or so in a box. Here is an example, with an answer, for the competency 'team working'. The space allowed would be appropriate for graduate recruitment, but for more experienced recruitment you may need to offer more.

TEAM WORKING

Please tell us about a time you worked in a team. Try to cover: a short description of the team and its goals; your role in the team; how you realized that other team members needed motivating; what exactly you did; what the result was.

In undertaking my Queen's Scout award I was part of a small group. I volunteered to be group leader for the planning of a gruelling five day expedition in the Cairngorms. This involved (i) assessing my team's capabilities and (ii) building morale within the group. I did this through (i) arranging fitness and map-reading tests, and (ii) stressing the benefits of completing the award, and the sense of fulfilment we would all get. Due to unforeseen weather conditions, we became lost and one of the team became rather tearful. I comforted him, and carried his pack for a while until we found our way again. Whilst on the expedition I built closer relationships between other members of the team by encouraging people to take on tasks together, such as finding wood for the camp fire. The result was successful completion of our fifty mile hike.

We describe how the answer would be marked later in the chapter. Application forms ensure that the information required by the employer is presented in a uniform way. Competencies are but one way of providing the structure which will deliver uniformity (although, of course, that can never be guaranteed; we have all come across applicants who can subvert any application form, self-defeating though it is to do so).

Not the least benefit of this approach is that the examples given can be used as a basis for further prompting during the competency-based interview (see Chapter 7). It is asking a lot of candidates to think up on the spot examples of 'a time when they worked in a team successfully'. To get around this, interviewers can use the example given in the application form as a way of moving forward.

The example question above is quite open-ended. Although a way of structuring the answer was suggested, through the 'points to cover', the structure was implicit rather than explicit. If it is thought that applicants need explicit structure in order that they can express themselves more clearly, then an overtly structured format like that in Table 5.1 can be used.

DECISION MAKING
In this job you need to be able to take responsibility for, and be prepared to defend, your decisions. Please describe a situation where you have had to make a difficult decision and explain it to other people.

What was the situation and the factors affecting it?

What were the consequences of getting it wrong or avoiding it?

How did you explain it?

How did you deal with any resistance?

What was the result?

Table 5.1   Structured Format Application Form Example

Finally, it is important to remember that a competency-based application form should also ask for other information deemed relevant, for example whether the applicant requires a work permit, holds a driving licence or has particular skills such as language skills.

Sifting competency-based application forms

So you are faced with 5000 completed competency-based application forms. OK, maybe the RJP didn't work but apart from screaming what do you do to reduce the numbers to manageable proportions? The screening process is one of matching the evidence given to the behavioural indicators you are looking for. This involves reading the entire application form (candidates may give you great evidence for 'Influencing', but in the box marked 'Interpersonal skills'), and then making a judgement on the quality of the evidence given.

A typical set of rules (indeed the ones adopted by Ros and Jack in the Fettercorn plc case study) is shown below.

Typical sifting rules

Each applicant should be given a rating on each competency of A, B or C according to the following rules:

'A' ratings
- strong evidence
- the answer is clear and directly answers the questions asked
- the answer contains most of the indicators (two-thirds or more)

'B' ratings
- acceptable evidence
- the answer gives an indication that evidence is present, but it is a little vague and needs to be explored more at interview
- the answer contains some indicators (approximately half)

'C' ratings
- poor evidence/lack of evidence
- the answer does not relate to the question
- the answer contains few indicators (one or two).

The initial shortlisting rule is as follows:

- Applicants who score no Cs should be invited to an interview.
- Applicants who score one C only should be put on hold for a period of one month.
- Applicants who score two or more Cs should be automatically rejected.

Now let us return to the actual answer we produced earlier. The competency was 'team working' (not one adopted by Fettercorn). A set of behavioural indicators is given below in Box 5.1.

BOX 5.1   BEHAVIOURAL INDICATORS FOR 'TEAM WORKING' AND 'PROBLEM ANALYSIS'

Team working

- Takes active role in the team.
- Motivates other team members.
- Supports team members in difficult times.
- Helps others to achieve team objectives.
- Helps people to work together in the team.
- Contributes to the achievement of the task.

Problem analysis

- Collects relevant information when solving problems.
- Avoids making assumptions.
- Is pro-active in identifying potential problems.
- Analyses information to identify patterns.
- Actively involves others where appropriate.
- Generates a range of options before making decisions.

This is how the answer would be scored according to the guidelines.

He or she took an active role, built morale, encouraged others, gained co-operation and contributed significantly to the completion of the tasks. Most of the indicators are hit, so it is an 'A'.

Here is another example. The competency this time is 'problem analysis'. The indicators are also reproduced in Box 5.1.

PROBLEM ANALYSIS

Please tell us about a time you had to solve a tricky problem. Try to cover: a short description of the problem; your approach to solving the problem; who else was involved; what exactly you did; what the result was.

As my university summer vacation approached I began the task of finding employment within the USA. After writing to various organizations I eventually acquired a job with a small US company but unfortunately due to unforeseen circumstances as I was about to depart, the offer of employment had to be cancelled. In a frantic search for another job I was left unsuccessful so I travelled to USA uncertain of my destination. On arriving in New York I made several enquiries within the student agency and via telephone to other students also in a similar position to myself who had arrived at an earlier date. My enquiries had to involve the availability of accommodation in addition to employment as I was to be alone, and also any transport links and distance from airports (in case all failed and there was a need to fly home). My enquiries were fruitless at first. Luckily, a friend of my Fathers' working for ABC Bank in New York contacted me and offered me a temping job.

Fortunately a very successful trip was made, and after three months and a short while spent travelling down the West Coast, I returned home.

This is a poor answer. See how much space is taken getting to the point, and when the point is reached, what does it amount to? A trying, even upsetting problem, but not a complex problem calculated to exercise the brain. The only indicators touched on are 'Actively involves others where appropriate' and (maybe) 'Generates a range of options before making decisions'. So a 'C' rating is given.

The application form and full sifting guidelines designed by Ros and Jack in the Fettercorn plc case study are reproduced at the end of the chapter.

The immediate discard technique

We began this chapter with mention of the immediate discard approach to sifting. For this to work with maximum efficiency it is necessary for the competencies to be presented on the form in a particular order, specifically, starting with the competency most closely related to overall performance on the job, then the next most closely related, and so on. That way the sift has the sharpest cutting edge. But how to judge what the order should be? If there has been a job analysis then that will yield some clues. If you are fortunate enough to have the results of some previous validation then you can use that to gain pointers. An example would be some work one of us did on application forms for entry to the police service. There were six competencies covered on the application form and a pilot exercise had ascertained, using performance ratings on the volunteers who had filled out the form, how the competencies correlated with job performance. With this information at our disposal we were able to order the competencies on the revised form so as to achieve the most efficient sift. For what it is worth, the leading competency was *Reliability*, followed by *Calmness under pressure*.

Sifting time

A common objection to competency-based application forms is that they will take too long to sift. On the contrary; if you are applying the immediate discard technique strictly, then the process will be swift, for to knock out applicants on the first or second competency would take no longer than a minute. If you have included a relatively large number of competencies on the application form (say, six) then the sheer size of the task is likely to put off speculative applicants. In such cases, the number of returns will be reduced, but the quality of applicants will be high.

Should you decide not to use the immediate discard technique (if you have no grounds for ranking the competencies, or because you prefer to score the whole form anyway), then with four competencies expect to take three minutes per form. For experienced hires, you may have stringent technical requirements, for example knowledge of C++, or fluency in Mandarin. In such cases, application forms should be sifted against these criteria first, further reducing the time requirement. In line with the survey data reported earlier, we strongly recommend training for sifters, and also double marking with checks to ensure consistency. A worked example is provided in Box 5.2 based on the Fettercorn situation.

Of course, you could always sift out purely on more obvious yet in our view irrelevant characteristics such as colour of ink used to complete the form, whether the writing is neat, or whether applicants cross their sevens. However, we feel that extra effort put in at the stage where you have the most people to choose from will pay dividends later.

BOX 5.2   SIFTING AT FETTERCORN

Ros and Jack expected to receive 200 completed application forms. Based on a six-competency form, their estimations for sifting time per form were as follows:

- discarded after one or two competencies – 1 minute
- discarded after three or four competencies – 2 minutes
- discarded after five or six competencies – 5 minutes.

They expected 40 per cent of forms to be discarded after two competencies, 40 per cent to be discarded after four, and 20 per cent to make it to the end. Based on these figures, the total time required to sift the forms would be 6 hours 10 minutes, or one day of Ros's time.

BIODATA

The second kind of application form uses biographical data to arrive at conclusions about likely future performance in a job. It is called 'biodata', or sometimes a weighted application blank. The answer format is usually multiple choice, so the form is susceptible to machine marking, which in terms of time is an advantage. A question might be:

Did your parents:

(a) Always help you with your school work?

(b) Usually help you with your school work?

(c) Seldom help you with your school work?

(d) Never help you with your school work?

Or, more objectively:

How many houses did you own by the age of 25?

(a) 0

(b) 1

(c) 2

(d) >2.

The usefulness of biodata needs to be queried. For some time it has been clear that hard data – 'objective and verifiable' – are more stable and reliable over, say, a five year period, than soft data – 'subjective and unverifiable'[4]. Thus, variables like highest educational qualification and birth order are preferred to, shall we say, position on capital punishment or whether your parents helped you with your school work. In the USA biodata has been shown to be used successfully to predict success as research engineer, oil industry research scientist, pharmaceutical industry researcher, bus driver and police officer[5].

If biodata is so effective, then why would we want to use a competency-based approach in preference? The answer lies in the scoring method applied to biodata. A scoring key is developed which weights answers so as to produce maximum differentiation between successful and less successful performers (as judged later in the job). Thus, if number of volunteer activities and birth order position are (among other variables) strongly associated with success in the job, then they are weighted up in the equation. If religious affiliation and marital status have no bearing, then these are weighted down, or not at all.

Developing a scoring key for biodata therefore is a thoroughly *empirical* affair, perhaps too empirical in the eyes of its critics. It doesn't matter *why* an item differentiates successful estate agents from unsuccessful, only that it does. Some psychologists have attempted to uncover underlying 'psychologically meaningful personal history variables'[6], but these are really only fishing expeditions, one step removed from dustbowl empiricism.

One factor which restricts the use of biodata is the need for large throughputs of applicants so as to be able to derive a scoring key empirically. This means that only the really large employers of people like the Civil Service can entertain it. The EDB survey reports that only 5% of employers use it as a regular part of the selection process for any job type.

In the past, the Civil Service has shown a keen interest in biodata, at least in its research programme. The Recruitment Research Unit (forerunner of Research and Assessment Services) found that candidates with high biodata scores, but test scores below the threshold, performed as well at the Civil Service Selection Board (CSSB) as other candidates invited on the basis of above-threshold test scores[7]. Their report suggested that this is because biodata picks up interpersonal skills and non-cognitive characteristics such as motivation, which the test scores obviously cannot do. Further development of the biodata instrument, the report concluded, might focus on measures of spare-time interests and organizational activities.

Given what was said earlier, it is somewhat ironic that biodata should be commended for tapping into 'softer' areas even if the motives for doing so (enriching selection data) are obviously sound. The point we would wish to make is that the competency-based approach already provides what extended biodata might give. It *is* intended to tap into competencies like interpersonal skills and motivation; it *does* invite applicants to draw on their spare-time and organisational activities.

We talked earlier of the dangers of cloning implicit in the competency-based approach. It will be apparent that with biodata those dangers are even greater. By its nature, an empirical scoring key is a device for producing clones, or at least excluding those who are different. It is freely conceded by those who have examined biodata closely that its validity shrinks over time, that no one knows which items will 'hold up' over time, and that, in a phrase, biodata is 'frequently caught in time'[8]. Of course, the same might be said of the competency-based approach but at least some safeguards against reproducing the past exist, as we pointed out in Chapter 2, when we talked about 'visioning' as a part of competency development.

Biodata and equal opportunities

Biodata also causes concern, particular concern, on the equal opportunities front. One example is that it has been found necessary to use different scoring keys for males and females[9]. It is also the case that items like sex, race, disability, convictions, height and weight, marital status, etc., which a biodata designer might want to include on the form, are definitely contentious and could be the focus of litigation if it could be shown that a selection decision hinged on them. Even questions on leisure pursuits and spare-time activities could prove objectionable, particularly in light of the Disability Discrimination Act (1996). Such questions might also contribute to 'subtle' discrimination, for example if particular ethnic groups are in general less privileged and so less likely to have had opportunities to undertake particular activities. Mike Smith and Ivan Robertson[10] found that applicants greatly disliked biodata inventories, calling them inaccurate and unfair. Note that the competency-based approach merely suggests that applicants might want to draw on leisure pursuits when framing their answers; they are not asked point-blank about them.

Biodata and honesty

Biodata measures are definitely fakeable. Overstating salary, and calling part-time work full-time, are common ploys. In principle, all biodata answers can be checked (by positive vetting) but employees know that this can take a long time and that many potential employers will not bother to run thorough checks. Hence they can risk faking. Much the same can be said about the competency-based approach, except that faking is harder work (you have to make up and embellish stories and make sure it all hangs together).

At the time of writing, we are designing a new competency-based application form for entry to the police service. To deter faking we are asking that each answer be vouched for by a named person. Since it is the police they are applying to, we reckon that would-be fakers will think twice before perjuring themselves!

CVs

The key difference between a CV and an application form lies in who has the control. In the application form, the organizations calls the shots; with the CV, the individual decides what to put. That said, it is becoming more common for people to structure their CVs along competency lines, and to that extent sifters are assisted (providing the competencies are the right ones).

However, the EDB survey notes that organizations who are keen to promote equal employment opportunities, notably those in the public sector, are particularly likely to reject the CV as a method of application, because they see them as a source of unwelcome discrimination through the allure to selectors of (probably irrelevant) information applicants want to supply. When the two of us were working for the Council of Legal Education, sifting applicants to train as barristers, we came across an applicant who was very concerned to communicate that he was a serving MP, and that for this reason alone he should certainly make it through the sifting; indeed he more or less defied us on paper to turn him down!

That said, the two most recent innovations in application forms both revolve around CVs and new technology. The first is use of the Internet. There are now several Internet sites which post job vacancies, and which hold CVs for companies to trawl through. An example is the way the Open University in the UK used the Internet to fill a position[11]. Some sites even provide search facilities to help companies match skill sets to vacancies.

The obvious advantage of using the Net is that the whole recruitment process is speeded up – adverts can bring in relevant CVs the same day. Also the process is cheaper than newspaper advertising – of the order of 10 to 20 per cent. The downside, as experienced recently by a large energy company known to us, is that it is almost *too* easy to send speculative CVs. This company received around 5000 speculative applications per month, of which 90 per cent were inappropriate, seriously so in most cases.

Perhaps employers have to learn these things for themselves. Meanwhile, Net providers like JobServe are reporting 21,000 job hunters using its services, and PeopleBank say they are holding around 85,000 CVs. At the moment, the bulk of Internet recruitment in the UK seems to be, naturally enough, for IT jobs. However, in the USA, Internet recruitment is an established method for a variety of job disciplines, and this is likely to be the case in the near future in the UK[12] – just beware junk applications.

The second innovation has arrived in the shape of sophisticated technology to sift CVs electronically[13]. Although it is less commonly found in the UK, 40 per cent of the top 100 firms in the USA use CV scanning software. The two key players in the market are both American – Resumix and Restrac – and after opening offices in the UK recently, both are making ground. For example, the BBC has decided to use Restrac both to save time recruiting externally, and to redeploy staff internally. Although expensive (circa £50,000), these systems can handle huge volumes of CVs – Australian recruitment company Morgan & Banks claims to be able to search 300,000 CVs in 10 seconds. The programs work by highlighting key skills (key words) which have been pre-identified. They are also, of course, truly blind in the way they sift – what we call the Patel–Evans problem (see next section) would not occur with CV scanning. Disadvantages are that the systems seem more suited to screening for technical skills. Although they could be programmed to search for competency key words, it is unlikely that the artificial intelligence is sophisticated enough to rate the *degree* of competency, which is what we ask human sifters to do.

FAIRNESS IN THE APPLICATION PROCESS

The EDB survey reports that more than a third of employers that use application forms (and that means more or less everybody) have made changes to them in the past two years, most recently to take account of the Disability Discrimination Act, which came into force on 2 December 1996. These changes are a matter of seeking more information from applicants about whether they have a disability, the nature of the disability and, in some cases, what (if any) special needs they might have. Such questions are usually asked in a detachable equal opportunities monitoring questionnaire, not available to selectors in case it might influence them.

Other reasons given for changing application forms also relate to equal opportunities issues, such as removing questions relating to children and marital status. Altogether, the EDB survey reports, more than seven out of 10 employers that have made changes to their forms have done so, at least in part, for reasons of equality.

Then there is what you might call 'everyday' discrimination. Perhaps it is not meant maliciously, but it happens all the same. It can be illustrated by what might be called the 'Patel-Evans' problem. A researcher sent speculative letters of application purporting to come from 'applicants' John Evans and Sanjay Patel. The letters went to 100 top UK companies. The upshot was (you guessed it) that Evans was better treated than Patel. It was not that Patel was badly treated, just that Evans received more favourable treatment, both in terms of quantity and quality of responses. The researcher[14] also studied how these companies stood on public commitment to equal opportunities and concluded that a gap exists between company policy and practice. How often has that been said? As we write, the British Armed Services have been heavily censured for failing to act against racism[15]. The Navy was especially singled out. It has an 'excellent' statement of equal opportunities, the report said, but one which was 'not matched by day-to-day understanding or practice'. Everyday or casual racism is a canker which can be expected to permeate every aspect of selection unless those in charge are extraordinarily vigilant.

SUMMARY

All three techniques – the competency-based form, biodata and the CV – rely on the proposition that the best guide to future performance is the past. The difference between them operationally is that the competency-based approach seeks to make rational, and *transparent*, connections between what the job or role will require (the job specification), and what the person has to offer. Providing the competencies have been defined with the future in mind (see Chapter 2), the competency-based method has a built-in way of coping with change – tell me what you did in the past and I will tell you if it will be useful in future.

With biodata you do not get that assurance. This is because it mimics – literally – the characteristics associated with successful performers in the past. It does not matter what those characteristics were, and how bizarre they might appear, if you have or do not have them now, then you are predicted to be a successful performer. In that sense, biodata is far from being transparent. The most worrying aspect of biodata from our perspective however is the potential for their use to impact adversely on certain groups of applicants such as disabled people, ethnic minority applicants and women.

Competency-based application forms, or rather the scoring schemes, can cope with all kinds of data, quantified or not. The validity of the scoring scheme, and the method of sifting, derive from the job analysis which specified the competencies, and their relative importance. If you were looking for a halfway house between biodata and the competency-based application form, as exhibited here, and we are sometimes asked for this, then it would be in a streamlined machine-scorable tickbox form, where what has to be endorsed are the behavioural indicators corresponding to each competency. But then we might find the same objections to being put on the spot as were encountered with biodata. As things stand, it seems best to leave the choice of what experiences to report to the applicant.

Finally, the use of CVs whilst on the surface retains the link between past and future performance, it is up to the human resource professional to make that link, and that could involve a huge amount of work. CVs also leave the choice of what experiences to report to the applicant. However, they do so in an unstructured way, again creating more work for the HR professional. As with biodata, there are potential equal opportunity implications, although standardization of sifting through computer-based key-word searches may, we stress may, help to mitigate fears. CVs can be a useful addendum to the recruitment process, particularly for senior jobs or for particularly technical jobs, but for large scale recruitment they are too much work, although the advent of scanning software could change all that.

FETTERCORN plc – A CASE STUDY

Whilst the advert had produced a large number of requests for application forms, it resulted in substantially fewer *completed* application forms.

'This is a great result,' Jack had said at the time but Ros was not too sure until she saw the quality of those who did apply. 'These people are great – really high calibre. The careful targeting must have had some impact.'

Jack was happy. He had made a stand early on in the design process. Ros had been very keen to use the immediate discard technique, but wanted to worry about the sifting rules and principles once they had sent out the terms. From past experience, Jack knew this was a false economy.

'You need to decide which order to put the competency questions on the application form, so that you discard those who fail the most important hurdle quickly, hence saving yourself time and money. You have the results of the competency analysis, and they gave a clear order of importance – "Achievement drive" correlated most highly with job performance, closely followed by "Influencing" and "Analysis". Using these three competencies in that order will definitely save you time in the long run.'

After some heated debate, Ros had finally bitten the bullet.

'Great, that's agreed then. Who is going to revise the form? . . . Oh, I see.' Jack reformatted the application form as instructed. The first three questions and the sifting guidelines are reproduced below.

FETTERCORN plc

Application form – Competency section

We are looking for evidence that you have the following competencies required in this job:

- achievement drive
- influencing
- analysis
- learning ability
- interpersonal skills
- planning and organizing.

Please give one or two examples from your recent (last five years) experience when responding to each question. Examples may be from work, education, leisure or voluntary activities.

When answering the questions, remember:

- Give one or two examples of what you actually did. Please be specific about your contribution.
- Do not give examples of things you are aware of but did not have any active involvement in.
- Be concise. Keep to the space provided and do not go into unnecessary details.

The information you provide will be used as a basis for deciding whom to shortlist for the next stage of the selection process. If you are successful here, be prepared to be questioned in depth on the examples you provide.

Achievement drive

Please give an example of when you achieved something difficult. Please cover: what the objective was; any obstacles you encountered; how you overcame them; how you felt about these obstacles; what the outcome was.

Influencing

Please give us an example of when you persuaded someone to do something for you. Please cover: what the stakes were; what the consequences of failure would have been; what exactly you did; what the outcome was.

Analysis

Please describe a complex problem you have tackled outlining in detail how you set about solving it. Please cover: how you identified the problem, what information you gathered, what analysis you carried out, the options/priorities you considered, your rationale for doing what you did; what the outcome was.

FETTERCORN plc

Application form sifting guidelines

* Each of the questions on the form is designed to elicit evidence on one particular competency. However, evidence for any competency may be found in any box, and if so should be included in your assessment.

* Each competency should be assessed using the following rating scale:
  A: Strong evidence
  B: Acceptable evidence
  C: Poor evidence

* Behavioural indicators are provided for each of the competencies. These will help you award a rating for each competency.

Instructions

* Every form should be given due consideration. At times it can become tedious and extremely hard work but for fairness's sake it

is essential that all applications are rated using a consistent approach.

- Ratings should be given on the following basis:

'A' ratings – strong evidence
- — the answer is clear and directly answers the questions asked
- — the answer contains most of the indicators (two thirds or more)

'B' ratings – acceptable evidence
- — the answer gives an indication that evidence is present, but it is somewhat vague and needs to be explored more at interview
- — the answer contains some indicators (approximately half)

'C' ratings – poor evidence/lack of evidence
- — the answer does not relate to the question
- — the answer contains few indicators (one or two)

- If you find the writing illegible, ask another sifter to take a look and verify whether or not the writing can be read. Applicants should not be eliminated because of poor handwriting.

- The initial shortlisting rule is as follows:

Applicants who score no Cs should be invited to an interview.

Applicants who score one C only should be put on hold for a period of one month.

Applicants who score two or more Cs should be automatically rejected.

- If by applying the shortlisting rule you achieve more applicants than it is practical to handle at the next stage of the selection process, secondary shortlisting should be carried out by applying a more stringent rule, e.g. an 'A' in each of the three key competencies. This rule must be applied consistently for all applicants.

- For each applicant you have rejected make a note of your reasons in the final column of the screening summary sheet (not reproduced here).

REFERENCES

1. Employee Development Bulletin (1997). The state of selection: An IRS survey. *EDB 85*.
2. Keenan, T. (1995). Graduate recruitment in Britain: a survey of selection methods used by organisations. *Journal of Organisational Behaviour,* **16**, 303–317.
3. Herriot, P. and Wingrove, J. (1984). Decision processes in graduate pre-selection. *Journal of Occupational Psychology,* **57**, 169–171.
4. Shaffer, G.S., Saunders, V. and Owens, W.A. (1986). Additional evidence for the accuracy of biographical data: Long term retest and observed ratings. *Personnel Psychology,* **39**, 791–809.
5. Reilly, R.R. and Chao, G.T. (1982). Validity and fairness of some alternative employee selection procedures. *Personnel Psychology,* **35**, 1–62.
6. Mitchell, T.W. and Klimoski, P.M. (1982). Is it rational to be empirical? A test of methods of scoring biographical data. *Journal of Applied Psychology,* **71**, 311–317.
7. Bethell-Fox, C.E., Cureton, R.N. and Taylor, J.A. (1988). The effectiveness of biodata in pre-selection for the Appointments-in-Administration competition. *RRU Report No 37*. London: Civil Service Commission.
8. Gunter, B., Furnham, A. and Drakeley, R. (1993) *Biodata*. London: Routledge.
9. Cook, M. (1988). *Personnel Selection and Productivity*. Chichester: John Wiley.
10. Smith, M. and Robertson, I.T. (1993). *The Theory and Practice of Systematic Personnel Selection (2nd Edition)*. London: Macmillan.
11. Kiceluk, A. (1996). The net that helps you fill vacancies. *People Management,* 30 May, 34–36.
12. Bird, J. (1997). Recruitment on-line. *Human Resources,* March/April, 21.
13. Sheppard, G. (1997) Screen test. *Personnel Today,* March, 28–29.
14. Noon, M. (1993). Racial discrimination in speculative application: Evidence from the UK's top 100 firms. *Human Resource Management Journal,* **3**, 35–47.
15. Rodrigues, J. and Brown, H. (1997). *Review of Ethnic Minority Initiatives*. London: Office of Public Management.

Competency-based interviewing I: Principles

6

Our purpose in this chapter is to discuss the various types of interview available for use in the recruitment and selection process. We then discuss fairness issues, leaving the practical issues of implementing a competency-based structured interview to the next chapter.

FETTERCORN plc – A CASE STUDY

Ros looked a little troubled. She thought she'd go over the issues one more time, as she still found it a little difficult to believe.

'So, Jack, you're telling me that despite being the most popular method of selection by far, interviews are pretty blunt tools, prone to bias, and we don't really know what it is they measure?'

'That's right,' Jack grinned. He loved being able to make such clear cut statements – they were rarely possible in the world of selection and recruitment.

'Interviews are not perfect – they never have been and they never will be. How can they be? They are simply one or two people making a judgement about another person's potential to work effectively in an incredibly complex environment. We can never deliver perfection – 100 per cent accuracy – and we should never promise it. Nor would we want it – what sort of world would that be? But we can do everything possible to maximize the effectiveness of every method we use, including the interview, and minimize possible bias.'

'So why are they used so much?' asked Ros, who was starting to wonder whether she needed an interview after all.

'It gives you, the interviewer, the security of having seen the candidate face-to-face. It gives the candidate the opportunity to put their case to a representative of the organization and to make some judgements about whether they want to work there or not. Apart from anything else, people have come to expect it, and would be disappointed if they didn't get it. The key is, if you're going to have an interview, and I think you are, then you've got to do it right.'

'OK,' said Ros. 'Start earning your money. What do I do? . . .'

EVERYONE USES INTERVIEWS

Interviews retain their universal appeal as a selection tool. Indeed, for many people, the interview is synonymous with selection. When someone says they are going for an interview, they mean they are going for a job, but when someone says they are going for a test, they are going for a test.

Two 1996 surveys of employers confirm the ubiquity of the interview, and that it really counts. In one survey[1], four out of five employers said that interviews were the most important part of their recruitment process. In the other, the EDB survey carried out by the IRS[2], all but one of the employers surveyed used interviews as a method of selecting staff. It is also the method employers most depend on when making decisions, although there are signs that this may be changing towards less reliance on the interview. Whereas in its 1991 survey, when the IRS reported 85 per cent of employers giving prime place to interviews, in 1996 that figure had fallen to 69 per cent. Even so, employers would not lightly sacrifice the interview's unique acceptability to candidates. People need the reassurance of being able to put their best foot forward in a face-to-face situation – 'if you can just get in to see the interviewer you can tell your whole story'[3].

DIFFERENT TYPES OF INTERVIEW

Sometimes it seems as if there are 57 varieties of interview. This is because academics and consultants have come up with their own 'brands' to describe essentially similar interview processes. There are, variously, the behaviourally-based criterion interview, the structured interview, the competency-based structured interview, the behavioural interview, the patterned behavioural description interview, and the structured behavioural interview. As far as we are concerned, these are essentially the same process.

To simplify the picture somewhat, let us make some clear distinctions. We shall discuss the interview under the following headings:

- the purpose of the interview
- structured versus unstructured interviews
- three types of structured interviews
- technology / format.

The purpose of the interview

Different types of interview can be used at different stages of the recruitment process for different purposes. There are at least three purposes
interviews can intentionally serve in the recruitment and selection process:

- initial screening
- further screening / in-depth assessment
- information giving / PR.

Some organizations use interviews as an initial screen of candidates.
When there are large volumes of candidates, this may even be done over
the telephone. The EDB survey confirms that telephone screening is most
likely to be used by large volume recruiters. It is, however, on the increase.
Thirty-five per cent (35%) of current users have introduced it in the past
two years.

University campus interviews are an example where *further screening*
might be done using an interview. At this stage, there are fewer candidates, initial screening having been accomplished previously by telephone
interview or application form. Such interviews usually take about 45
minutes, and allow information to be collected on a small number of
competencies – perhaps those identified through research as the most
critical, or as the most difficult to develop further.

Information giving is most likely to occur at second interview or at an
assessment centre (along with specific information events such as open
evenings or presentations). It may seem odd to be talking about an
interview as information *giving* (isn't an interview something someone
does to someone else?) but we have in mind Peter Herriot's still somewhat
radical idea that the interview should be removed from the front line of
selection, where suspect validity and reliability make it a menace, and
used instead as a medium for negotiation with those with whom the
organization wishes to discuss future employment[4]. In this kind of interview, the power balance between interviewer and candidate should be
more equal, or if anything in favour of the candidate for the first time. The

candidate must decide whether they want to work for this organization or not, and this is an opportunity to discuss the 'psychological contract' explicitly. If the candidate is made an offer, the decision as to whether to accept will depend to an extent on the impression he or she forms of the organization, and this will be based in large part on the image projected by the interviewer(s). There is good evidence in the literature[5], and certainly anecdotally, that applicants take into account how they were treated at interview when deciding whether or not to accept a job offer. Hence, the interview also has a great deal of PR power.

Structured versus unstructured interviews

This is the most important distinction to make. In truth, it does not really matter what your interview is called as long as it is structured or, rather, as long as it is not unstructured. There are few things that psychologists agree on, but one of them is that unstructured interviews do not work. Many studies have shown the predictive validity of unstructured inter-views to be around zero[6], which is like tossing a coin. And as if that was not bad enough, unstructured interviews are likely to have negative effects. Consider the archetypal unstructured interview. The managing director invites you in for a 'chat'. He or she asks you about your background, where you went to school or university, what your family does, and why you want this job. From this he or she forms an impression of whether you have the potential to perform effectively in the job. Wrong. What they actually form an impression of is (i) whether you are similar to them, and (ii) whether they like you, which in turn is heavily influenced by (i). This of course can lead to a continuous reinforcement of the status quo, recruitment of clones, and indirect discrimination against applicants from under-represented groups. For a pertinent anecdote, see Box 6.1.

For all their merits, structured interviews do not get round this problem completely. In any social interaction, people will form judgements about other people based on their stereotypes, their expectations and their own insecurities. What you *can* do, by structuring the interview, is to cut down on such problems. This is done by obliging interviewers to concentrate on gathering information which has previously been identified, through job or competency analysis, as important for effective job performance. This takes some getting used to at the beginning. As a process it is rather like asking someone who hitherto has been accustomed to watching a team game of some sort without any introspection whatsoever, just watching the game as a spectacle, to start taking account of who is actually doing what, and to whom, and how often. Maybe the tall blond guy caught the eye, and you are inclined to say 'He was good', but what did he actually

---

BOX 6.1   SIMILAR TO ME?

Some years ago, the second author attended a milk round assessment centre for a multinational FMCG manufacturer. The assessors were drawn from the many operating companies within the group and the first thing they did at the beginning of the day was to introduce themselves. The chair of the assessors, who was also Chairman of one of the largest operating companies, introduced himself, saying how he went to grammar school, played in the school orchestra, and played rugby. When the time came for the candidates to introduce themselves, the author was lucky enough to be able (truthfully) to say that he had also attended a grammar school, played in the orchestra, and played rugby. For the rest of the day, the Chairman was extremely friendly, swapping conspiratorial smiles and nods during the interview. The author got the job, but of course this might have been totally on merit . . .

---

accomplish? It is the analytical approach over the holistic that needs to be encouraged.

Three types of structured interview

The three most commonly encountered kinds of structured interview are:

- the biographical interview
- the backward looking interview
- the forward looking interview.

All can be made to relate directly to competencies, although it is much easier to do this with the last two.

In the *biographical interview*, the interviewer takes the candidate through their CV, exploring their experience, their motivations for job changes or other significant decisions, and their aspirations. The interview is structured by chronology, but it is very important to have a clear set of criteria (such as competencies) against which to evaluate the information gained. If not, this can quickly become an unstructured interview – 'Oh, I see you hunted giant mallard in Tajikistan; I bet that was exciting.' This is the kind of interview often favoured by headhunters who reckon they know how to find 'the right kind of chap'. As often as not, loose and unstructured advertisements breed loose and unstructured interviews.

The *backward looking interview* sounds a little strange, but of all the interview formats is generally reckoned to be the most reliable and best predictor of future success in the job. Like the application form it is based on the premise that the best predictor of future behaviour is past performance. Indeed nearly all of the 'branded' interviews referred to in the introduction to this chapter fall into this category.

The backward-looking interview lends itself extremely well to assessing a person against a competency framework. Say, for example, that you want to assess someone's planning and organizing ability. The interviewer would ask the candidate 'Can you give me an example of a time when you have planned a particularly complex project?' The candidate would then begin to recount an example, and the interviewer would pick up on particular issues as they emerged–'Why did you do that? Did the project suffer any unforeseen problems? How did you handle them?' The questions are designed to provide specific behavioural evidence of what the candidate has done in the past. By asking about real events, the skilled interviewer should be able to identify behavioural patterns, as well as whether the candidate is simply 'talking a good game'. The candidate's answers are later analyzed and marked against the behavioural indicators relating to that competency. We shall examine various ways of doing this later.

Forward looking interviews are like the backward looking variety with, as you would expect, one important difference – they look forward to what a candidate might do. Instead of asking 'Can you give me an example of . . .', they ask 'Consider this situation . . . what would you do?' Because of this format, they are usually referred to as *situational interviews*. Again, they fit easily into a competency framework. However, they are quite resource-intensive to design; also the interviewers need at least three model answers to each question (a good answer, an OK answer and a poor answer).

It has been suggested that the situational interview, in particular, is no more than an orally administered cognitive ability test[7]. That position seems to have been abandoned with the emergence of evidence that interviews can contribute incrementally to validity over and above ability tests, even if we do not always know what they are measuring[8]. Some Canadian investigators[9] showed that a situational interview is more likely to be a measure of *practical* than traditional intelligence, and pointed to the salience of prior work experience and the way it shapes tacit knowledge. That is why situational interviews can be particularly useful when faced with the task of recruiting from a set of very experienced people where it might be difficult to distinguish between their answers to a backward looking interview.

In evaluating what we are saying, you should be aware that recent studies have shown[10] that both past-oriented and future-oriented questions can deliver incremental validity but that the past questions are somewhat more effective[11]. Unless, as noted above, you are dealing with very experienced people, the *backward looking* interview is preferred.

Technology/format

A further distinction can be made, which can be called technology, or perhaps format. We look at two issues:

- number of interviewers
- technology.

Number of interviewers

Consider the following questions. Which is better, a panel of interviewers, or a one-to-one arrangement? Should there be a separate note-taker, or should interviewers take their own notes? In both cases, the answer is 'it all depends'. Panel interviews have advantages in that the greater number of judges boost reliability, but have disadvantages in that they are resource intensive, can be intimidating, and can look terrible if not well organized.

In terms of note-taking, if you can afford the luxury of a dedicated note-taker, then this frees up the interviewer to spend more time building rapport with the candidate, and thinking up their next question. It does however double the resource requirement.

Technology

Technological considerations relate to the media to be used for the interview. Alternatives to face-to-face interviews include the telephone interview and the video-conferencing interview. Telephone interviews are becoming more popular, but have received little empirical attention. One recent investigation[12] found that, compared with face-to-face interviews, telephone interviews always resulted in a lower rating of candidates, presumably because there was no visual evidence to moderate the rating (always remember that, for better or worse, what you say is far less important than how you look, or even how you say it, which itself raises a big question mark against interviews). The implication of this is that you should not mix both types of interview in the same recruitment exercise.

In the USA, video-conference interviews are becoming popular with organizations interviewing undergraduates on campus. Although more research is needed, this technique clearly has economic advantages. We suspect it will not be too long before people are being interviewed over the Internet using PC-mounted video cameras, having already located the job on the World Wide Web and submitted an application via e-mail as described in the last chapter.

FAIRNESS AND THE INTERVIEW

Just because something is popular, does not mean it is right, or good. As regards fairness, the spotlight recently has been trained on tests and personality questionnaires, but some of us have been worried about the *fairness* of interviews for a long time. Take, for example the Brent and Coventry Healthcare industrial tribunal cases, where the first author was the expert witness for UNISON. In both cases, the suspicion was that unfairness was due to the tests, but the first author was sure it was the interview process which was doing the damage. The mistake – a classical logical fallacy – is to suppose that just because tests are being rubbished, the interview is therefore sound.

This readiness to ignore the objective (tests) in favour of the subjective (interview) is odd. It is a bit like rejecting the alarm clock in favour of the fellow who knocks on your window, who himself relies on an alarm clock to get up. However maladroitly tests are used, and they are, it is still the case that an interview is inherently less objective simply because tests are unarguably *blind*, and the interview is not (remember, it's how you look, not what you say). An improving validity record (see above) has seen interviews attaining greater respectability, but let us not kid ourselves that problems of prejudice and bias have gone away.

Formal investigations into interview fairness

As if it, too, believed that interviews were suddenly unproblematical, the Commission for Racial Equality (CRE) in the UK has had much to say about tests in recent times, but has been curiously reticent about interviews. In the Eighties, it showed more interest. There were at least two formal investigations where the interview was targeted for attention. In one – the 1987 investigation into recruitment for chartered accountancy training[13] – the report notes how interviewers from accountancy firms would make comments about Asian candidates' apparent diffidence, such as 'lacking presence', 'lacking character or sparkle', or 'flat personality'. Another perception was that Asians were 'over eager', or 'trying to please too much'. There were several comments about the facial features of African candidates. It was noted that comments had also been made on white applicants' personality and appearance, but that these covered a broader range and appeared less often.

In a 1985 investigation, this time into the Polymer Engineering Division of Dunlop Ltd, Leicester[14], difficulties in communication was the theme. The investigators noted that they had found seven black or Asian applicants (six Asians and a West Indian) to be unsuccessful, either because of an inability to 'communicate' or an inability to answer questions at interview to the panel's satisfaction. Other black or Asian candidates were rejected because of a lack of experience, or lack of initiative and personality. White candidates were rejected for similar reasons (i.e. lack of initiative or understanding of the job), but none was rejected because of difficulties in communication.

That was not all. The investigation discovered that the selection interview given by Dunlop required applicants to use indirect, formal language in an unfamiliar, artificial context. They had to hypothesize, for example, in describing how they would deal with a particular problem (forward looking interview), and to give opinions on certain issues. To succeed in this, they had to understand and recognize the panel's intentions behind their questions and, in reply, use the right degree of abstract language and assertiveness. In contrast, the investigators found that spoken communication on the shop floor was of a different order, being direct, informal, short, unfamiliar or colloquial language, and with roles clearly defined.

The Dunlop investigators were satisfied that ethnic minority, and particularly Asian, applicants (being more likely not to have English as a first language), would be proportionately less able to comply with the oral and written communication requirements in the selection procedure. In a separate exercise, failed applicants whose first language was not English were asked typical interview questions supplied by Dunlop. Although there was not a great deal of difference between the responses of failed white and Asian applicants, nevertheless the investigators considered that the answers of the Asians were less immediately relevant and their intonation, grammar and choice of vocabulary rendered their replies more difficult to evaluate.

These candidates also found it more difficult to know what was expected of them in an interview, for example, in using the right amount of indirectness and assertiveness, particularly as the requirements of the selection procedure were not explicit; nor were reasons for particular interview questions and the qualities being assessed from the answers to these questions explained.

Those CRE reports are 10 years or more old now, but does anyone want to say that they are old hat, that they have been overtaken by events? No; interviewer bias has not gone away. A 1996 industrial tribunal (*Nwoke v. (1) Government Legal Service and (2) Civil Service Commissioners*[15]) found that an applicant for a post in the Government Legal Service had been discriminated against on grounds of both sex and race when she received a low mark for her interview. The tribunal expressed concern at the lack of consistency in the marking, and inferred from this that 'subjectivity played a large part in the assessment of individual candidates'. It is deeply depressing to still find interview panel members querying whether individuals will 'fit in'.

Note that a panel was operating. The 1996 EDB survey says (p.12) that the biggest single change since 1991 is the tendency to involve more selectors in the interview – 'the collective views of two or more selectors are now seen as more likely to reach a fair and correct decision'. Well, yes and no, or maybe. Panels can be swayed, and if they share the same bias(es) their decisions will converge very quickly.

On an even more extreme note than Ms Nwoke's case, another recent industrial tribunal (*Baptiste v. Westminster Press t/a Bradford & District Newspapers*[16]) concluded that a display sales manager who told a black candidate during the interview that it was not uncommon for her to use the phrase 'black b******' and that it was part of workplace banter had behaved in a discriminatory fashion. The thing to note about this case, apart from the gratuitous offensiveness and naivety of the sales manager, is that the company had an equal opportunities policy and code of practice in place. That, said the tribunal, was not sufficient for the employer to avoid liability for the manager's act. The implication is that a company keen to employ the rhetoric of equal opportunity may be just as guilty of disguising or ignoring the practice of equal opportunities as those companies that do not have an equal opportunities statement. The gulf between policy and practice – how often have we seen that?

This is the sort of thing that is (still) happening on the ground. The academic literature at large, in what is, surprisingly, a somewhat neglected area, can be read as indicating that there is not a problem. An American review of the mid-80s, and there is very little more recent, concluded that:

> 'current research evidence indicates that females and blacks are not adversely affected by interview recommendations relative to males and white applicants.'[17]

This review does add the rider that there are studies that may be contra-indicative when individuals are seeking *out-of-role* jobs (my italics). We wonder if this gives the game away. Much initial recruitment must, by definition, be out-of-role. Students applying for accountancy training are applying for out-of-role jobs. All promotions must be considered out-of-role, otherwise it cannot be a promotion (leaving aside recognition of de facto upgradings).

The trouble is that we still do not have a very good handle on what interviews might actually be measuring. To be technical, what construct validity do they have? Do they measure social skills, motivation, communication skills, etc., and how well do they do it? The best guess is that they measure sociability, for sure, and a mishmash of other attributes which are more or less predictive of job performance. The Hays survey[1] reported that 'unkempt appearance' and 'inability to look you in the eye' were most likely to put someone off a candidate. This can be read as code for 'not fitting in'.

As assessment professionals, we do our best to keep the interview honest. This involves establishing a structure and keeping to it, taking more or less verbatim notes, and using a rational and fair marking scheme, with trained assessors to operate it (see Box 6.2). More often that not, the interview is structured around the measurement of specific competencies shown to be relevant to the job in question. But we would never pretend that we were operating a sophisticated measuring device. Rather we are trying to collect sound, dependable evidence which can be mixed with other, 'harder', evidence.

SUMMARY

In this chapter, we have discussed the different types of interview available for use within a recruitment and selection process. We have pinpointed the *backward looking* competency-based interview as the most efficient, and have provided practical guidance on what such an interview might look like. We have also taken time to critically evaluate the fairness of interviews, and pointed out that, although interviews have received less attention recently, they still have the potential they have always had to be unfairly discriminatory. In the next chapter we shall return to Fettercorn plc to see how Ros got on with interviewing.

BOX 6.2   AVOIDING BIAS IN THE INTERVIEW

Improvements in selection interviewing are likely to be achieved by:

- Training interviewers not only on how to collect information but on how to evaluate it.
- Clarifying the objectives to be achieved in the interview.
- Seeing as much information as possible is collected about the vacancy before the interview.
- Ensuring that as much information as possible about the candidate is gathered before the interview.
- Trying to collect information about the candidate by other means in addition to the interview, e.g. selection tests.
- Providing interviewers with a structure or checklist for gathering information within the interview.
- Encouraging interviewers to take notes during the interview.
- Helping interviewers to monitor how their behaviour may be affecting the candidate.
- Encouraging interviewers to avoid reaching conclusions until all the information can be evaluated after the interview.
- Providing interviewers with a simple form for rating applicants on a few, clearly defined, characteristics.
- Establishing systems for interviewers to get feedback on their interview behaviour and on the decisions they have made.

REFERENCES

1. Hays Accountancy Personnel quoted in *The Times* 29.7.96.
2. Employee Development Bulletin (1997). The state of selection: An IRS survey. *EDB 85.*
3. Hakel, M.D. (1982). The employment interview. In Rowland, K.M. and Ferris, G.R. (Eds) *Personnel Management.* Boston, MA: Allyn & Bacon.
4. Herriot, P. (1989). Selection as a social process. In Smith, M. and Robertson, I.T. (Eds), *Advances in Selection and Assessment.* London: Wiley.
5. Harn, T.J. and Thornton, G.C. (1985). Recruiter counselling behaviours and applicant impressions. *Journal of Occupational Psychology,* **58,** 57–65.
6. Anderson, N.R. (1991). Eight decades of employment interview research: A retrospective meta-review and prospective commentary. *The European Work and Organisational Psychologist,* **2** (1), 1–32.
7. Campion, M.A., Pursell, E.D. and Brown, B.K. (1988). Structured interviewing:

Raising the psychometric properties of the employment interview. *Personnel Psychology*, **41**, 25–42.

8. McDaniel, M.A., Whetzel, D.L., Schmidt, F.L. and Maurer, S.D. (1994). The validity of employment interviews: A comprehensive review and meta-analysis. *Journal of Applied Psychology*, **79**, 599–616.

9. Durivage, A., St. Martin, J. and Barrette, J. (1995). Practical or traditional intelligence: What does the situational interview measure? *European Review of Applied Psychology*, **45**, 179.

10. Campion, M.A., Campion, J.E. and Hudson, J.P. (1994). Structured interviewing: A note on incremental validity and alternative question types. *Journal of Applied Psychology*, **79**, 998–1002.

11. Pulakos, E.D. and Schmitt, N. (1995). Experience-based and situational interview questions: Studies of Validity. *Personnel Psychology*, **48**, pp. 289–308.

12. Silvester, J., Haddleton, E., Anderson, N., Cunningham-Snell, N. and Gibb, A. (1997). Selecting personnel by telephone: A reliable alternative to face-to-face interviews. *Occupational Psychology Conference Book of Proceedings*, 143–149.

13. CRE (1987). *Formal investigation into chartered accountancy training*. London: Commission for Racial Equality.

14. CRE (1985). *Formal investigation into Dunlop Polymer*. London: Commission for Racial Equality.

15. *EOR Discrimination Case Law Digest* No. 28, Summer 1996.

16. *EOR Discrimination Case Law Digest* No. 30, Winter 1996.

17. Schmitt, N. and Noe, R.A. (1986). Personnel selection and equal employment opportunity. In Cooper, C.L. and Robertson, I.T. (Eds) *International Review of Industrial and Organisational Psychology*. Chichester: John Wiley.

Competency-based Interviewing II: Practice 7

The purpose of this chapter, which complements the last, is to go over the practical skills needed to conduct competency-based interviews effectively. Also provided, in the context of the case study, are some samples of the kind of documentation required for correct implementation.

We would be surprised if there were any readers of this book who have not had some experience of interviewing. Either you have been interviewed, or you have interviewed someone else, or both. It could be a counselling, appraisal, disciplinary, feedback, debriefing, media or selection interview. Whatever the situation, most people have experienced the interview process and, more significantly, believe they know what it is all about.

When we train managers to use competency-based interviews, we start by asking two simple questions:

> Q1. *Thinking back over the interviews you have been involved in (either as interviewer or interviewee), what went well?*

And then:

> Q2. *What went badly? What could have been done differently?*

Without fail, these questions will bring out the most important points to remember when interviewing. The key issues are summarized through the mnemonic OPQRST featured in Box 7.1*.

---

* Thanks to Binna Kandola for permission to use this mnemonic, which he devised.

BOX 7.1   THE KEY SKILLS OF INTERVIEWING

O   for   **OBJECTIVES** – be clear about what you need from the interviews.

P   for   **PREPARATION** – plenty of it for both interviewer and interviewees.

Q   for   **QUESTIONING** – open questions preferred and careful probing.

R   for   **RAPPORT** – without it you won't get the best out of the interviewees.

S   for   **STRUCTURE** – you must have an interview plan, and you must follow it.

T   for   **TAKING NOTES** – absolutely essential. Don't rely on your memory – you'll remember less than 10% of what you hear.

OBJECTIVES

If you are not clear about what you want to get out of an interview, you won't get it. Whilst this seems obvious, it is important. Remember the unstructured interview, or 'informal chat' – because the objective is unclear, the process loses focus. The TV programme *Face to Face* is a good example. When John Freeman ran it, he was like a dog with a bone. You knew he wanted to extract information from his guests that they did not want to give. Now, with Jeremy Isaacs, no one gives anything away, because he does not probe – not where it might hurt anyway. One of the great TV interviews was when Martin Bashir interviewed Princess Diana. He was well prepared, knew what he wanted to get out of it, and kept digging until he succeeded in giving viewers information they did not have before.

The main objective of the interview should be to *collect* relevant information. You do not *evaluate* the information during the interview. That comes afterwards. By relevant information, we mean relevant to the competencies you are trying to assess. In practice, this means gathering *specific examples* of what the candidate has actually achieved in the past and how they did it. Only by gathering specific behavioural examples can you evaluate the candidate against the competencies.

Other objectives

There are other objectives to pursue. For example:

- making sure the people you interview fully understand the job they are applying for
- treating everyone with the same professionalism and courtesy that you would like to experience if you were a candidate.

Never forget that interviews are a two-way process. It would be deeply disappointing (and costly) if you were to make an offer to a candidate, only to be rejected by them because they had formed a negative impression of your organization during the interview. The interview always has a public relations function.

PREPARATION

The foundation for a successful interview is preparation for both the interviewer and the candidate. When we do interviewer training courses, this is the one item which delegates always mention as something they need to work on in future.

Preparing the candidate

Put on the spot, it can be difficult for candidates to think up telling examples of their past behaviour. This is where the competency-based application form comes into its own. The examples candidates give on the form are perfect starting points for the interviewer. Thus, interviewers may spend some time questioning the candidate about the example already given, and then move on to ask for further evidence. The familiarity of the information given previously will help the interview to 'flow'.

Once in the interview, you can prepare the candidate by following these guidelines:

- introduce yourself
- put the candidate at ease
- say how long the interview will last
- explain the structure of the interview
- say that notes will be taken to enable a fair assessment to be made later

- check that they understand
- ask if they are ready to begin.

Preparing yourself

Interviewers have a great responsibility, because if they do not ask the questions, and give the candidate the opportunity to provide evidence of their success, then the candidate will be penalized through no fault of their own. When preparing yourself to interview candidates you should:

- read their application form or CV
- identify any issues which require clarification
- work out which aspects of the competencies will require extra probing
- choose your opening questions
- prepare additional questions to cover anything likely to be left over.

We often suggest interviewers use a preparation form with example questions, and spaces to write specific questions. Such a form is described in the case study at the end of the chapter.

QUESTIONING

Since the primary objective of the interview is to obtain evidence from the candidate, it follows that he or she should do most of the talking. Specifically, you should aim to have the candidate talking approximately 70 to 80 per cent of the time. The knack to this lies in the type of questions you ask.

Open questions

These questions enable candidates to provide facts and information, describe things, express feelings or opinions, etc. In short, they get candidates talking. For example:

Tell me about the duties in your present job.

> How did you deal with an irate member of the public?

Closed questions

> Did you enjoy your last job?
> Did you get on well with your supervisor?

In either case the candidate could answer 'yes' or 'no', and in both cases the answer would be a sufficient reply. Closed questions are useful for checking your understanding of answers, or checking specific facts, but are not good for getting candidates to open up.

Double-headed questions

These occur when two or more questions are asked in one go. For example:

> Why have you applied for this job, where do you see yourself in five years' time, and why do you want to leave your present job?

On these occasions, candidates will either focus on the questions they want to answer and ignore those which might be difficult or too revealing, or they might just forget one of the questions. Politicians are very apt to do this. Next time you watch Prime Minister's Question Time watch out for it. If you want to know the answers to each question, ask them one at a time.

Leading questions

This is where the answer to the question is given away in the question itself. This usually occurs where the interviewer prefaces the question with some information either from the job description or the person specification. For example:

> In this job you have to lick a lot of stamps. How do you feel about licking stamps?

or

> We are looking for somebody who can work to deadlines. How well do you work to deadlines?

With questions like these, you are playing straight into the hands of the experienced candidate or the ones who are good talkers. 'Licking stamps – I love it. I can never get enough of it. I would count it a poor day if I did not lick some stamps.' 'Deadlines – they're a doddle. I eat deadlines. If I didn't have deadlines, I couldn't get out of bed.' And so on.

In recent years an insidious form of the leading question has spread among TV interviewers like a virus. It is especially noticeable among sports commentators. 'How much enjoyment did you get from scoring the last minute winner?' 'How concerned are you that your leg has just been broken?' And so on. The 'How' question is usually recommended (you might have heard mention of the interviewer's three little friends, 'Why', 'What' and 'How'), but not the way these people use it. It is a travesty of questioning. It looks as if they were taught the virtues of the open question, and then spoilt it with the giveaway in the question.

Hypothetical questions

This is where the interviewer describes a situation to the candidate and asks them what they would do. Unless you are using a properly developed situational interview as described earlier, too many questions of this type should be avoided. This is because what a person says they will do in a given situation might be completely different from what they would actually do, and because you have no way of evaluating the answer consistently. It is much better to look back at how a person *has* handled similar situations in the past, rather than trying to see how they *might* handle a situation in the future. So, rather than asking, 'How would you deal with an irate customer if you were faced with one?', you might ask:

> Can you give me an example of when you had to deal
> with an irate member of the public?

Multiple-choice questions

This is the oral equivalent of a multiple-choice item in a written test. It is where the interviewer asks a question and provides the candidate with a number of answers to select from. For example:

> How did you find out about this job? Was it through
> the Job Centre, your careers teacher, an advertisement,
> a friend who works for the organization, or what?

Quite often the first part of the question (in this case, 'How did you find out about this job?') is good enough on its own.

Self-assessment questions

This is where the interviewer asks candidates to assess themselves. For example:

> Can you tell me why you think you are suitable for the job?

These are very difficult questions to answer, but again they also play into the hands of the smooth talker or experienced candidate. On the other hand, you already know what characteristics the successful applicant should have – the competencies that you have identified – so why not ask them specifically about these?

Probing questions – the funnel technique

It is not enough just to ask open questions. The answer to an open question will give you some information but it will not be enough usually to make an assessment of a candidate on any of the characteristics on a person specification. What is needed are further follow-up questions to probe a particular area in more depth.

One method for doing this is known as the funnel technique for probing (see Figure 7.1). You should begin by asking an open question which refers to something that the candidate has done in the past and which also relates to one of the competencies. Once you have an answer, pursue the candidate down the funnel (in the nicest possible way). You will not be able to do it with every question, because there is not enough time (15 minutes per competency is the maximum you will get), so try to reserve funnelling for those answers which are potentially revealing if followed up.

RAPPORT

Striking a rapport with the candidate is important. You are interested in hearing what they have achieved, and they will be in a better position to tell you (and to reveal aspects of themselves which they otherwise might not do) if they are relaxed. There are a number of ways in which an interviewer can strike up a rapport. These include finding some common

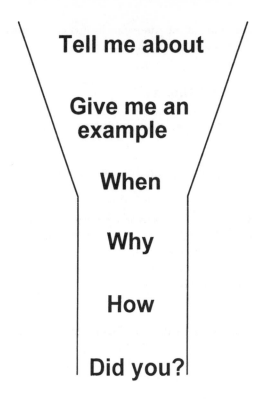

Figure 7.1   Probing – the funnel

ground (but not overdoing the friendliness thereby engendered), listening, and providing verbal and non-verbal clues.

Building rapport does not mean that you cannot question candidates closely, but it does mean avoiding the 'let's put them under pressure' approach. It is sometimes held that it is okay to put candidates under pressure at an interview because after all the job is stressful. The argument does not hold together at all – the job and the interview are not comparable. A sequence like (Q: Are you good under pressure? A: Yes. Q: Are you good with numbers? A: Yes. Q: What's 15 per cent of 75?) should be avoided.

Finding common ground

This is really in the nature of an 'ice-breaker'. You might spot something on the application form, or CV (if there is one). 'I see you like to go bungee jumping. I do too. Have you ever tried the North Face of the Eiger?' One of us was interviewing a marketing person recently. He had spotted that she had been responsible for marketing a certain soft drink. When he told her that he and his family loved that drink, couldn't get enough of it, she was thrilled. 'Let me send you a case – do you like the guava or the mango?' Needless to say, the case never arrived, but it was a good ice-breaker. Remember, you only need one, otherwise the interview can start to ramble, and if that happens it is your fault as the interviewer.

Listening

Interviewers should always concentrate on what the candidate is saying – what is called 'active listening'. The candidate is unloading a lot of information and the interviewer has to be able to recall it, use it, relate it to the competencies, relate it to what has gone earlier, check for inconsistencies, etc. Follow-up questions are, by definition, related to what the candidate has just said and in order to react the interviewer must obviously have paid attention not just to *what* is being said, but also the *way* in which it is being said, for example, the tone of the voice which is used.

Verbal cues

These include:

Reflecting back

This is where the interviewer asks a question which relates to something which the candidate may have said earlier on. For example:

> You mentioned just now that you enjoyed geography
> at college. Why was that?

Making links

This is similar to reflecting back, but it is used not so much to ask questions but to form links between one section of an interview and another. For example:

> Your reference to new technology takes us on neatly to
> the next phase of the interview, as I would like to ask
> you some questions about your experience of
> computer-aided manufacturing. Tell me about ...

Summarizing

Here the interviewer summarizes the information which has been gathered from the candidate and feeds it back. This serves a number of purposes. First of all, it shows the candidate that the interviewer has been paying attention and, secondly, it provides an opportunity for the interviewer to check that they have recorded and interpreted the information correctly. If the information is incorrect the candidate will have a chance to put the record straight. Summaries are best done as a matter of course throughout the interview, perhaps once or twice, and also at the end of the interview. In our interviewer training courses we test the adequacy of delegates' notes by asking them to summarize at the end. Usually, no notes equals no summary.

Non-verbal cues

Interviewers must not only listen but they must be seen to be listening. They have to communicate with their face, with gestures, with movements, which all indicate to the candidate that the interviewer is interested and is giving them maximum attention. Types of non-verbal cues which convey this message include nodding of the head, smiling, looking (but not staring) at the candidate, and occasional noises of encouragement such as 'hm, hm' (if that is the kind of noise you make).

Varieties of non-verbal behaviour which should be avoided include looking at your watch, continually looking down at your papers and not at the candidate, critical frowning, staring out of the window, and pointing with your finger at the candidate. If you feel a yawn coming on, yawn (covering your mouth, of course); do not try to suppress it and end up blowing out your cheeks. It looks even worse.

Occasionally, there will be times when there are mismatches between what the candidate is telling you and the way that they are acting in front of you, which may lead you to suspect that the information you are being given is not entirely accurate. This type of behaviour is known as non-verbal leakage. Rather than automatically assuming that the candidate is lying, you should use the opportunity to probe in more depth the area that is being discussed.

STRUCTURE

Working to a structure is a major step towards improving the quality of interviewing, as it helps to:

- ensure that nothing major is omitted
- keep track of how time is being used
- give candidates a sense of progress through the interview.

Most competency-based structured interviews are divided into three sections:

- introduction and general questions
- competency section where each competency is questioned in turn
- candidate's questions and close.

A typical interview covering six competencies should be expected to last around one and a half hours, with an average of fifteen minutes being spent on questioning each competency.

TAKING NOTES

Nothing is more important than taking notes, even preparation. Do not rely on memory, however good you think it is. Not for nothing is it said, 'A short pencil is more effective than a long memory.'

There are a number of points to bear in mind when taking notes:

- Do not take notes furtively – be open about it. Tell the candidate you will be taking notes, but do not do it in such a way that the candidate can see what is being written.
- Take as full a note as you possibly can without letting the note-taking process interfere with your interviewing technique. If that means only a short *aide-memoire*, so be it, as long as it is an *aide-memoire*.
- Be careful about when you write something down. Highly personal or adverse information should be noted when the conversation has moved on.
- Remember, your notes will be the only source of evidence that will enable you to justify your rating and ultimately the selection decision. Notes may be requisitioned in case of litigation. We have been appalled, but not surprised, at the state of notes produced in industrial tribunals.

MARKING THE INTERVIEW

Interviews can be marked just like application forms. To mark a competency-based interview, three things are needed:

- marking guidelines and behavioural indicators
- a summary rating form
- a rating scale.

Marking guidelines and behavioural indicators

These guidelines set out the process for marking the interview. The key steps are:

- wait until the interview is completed
- read all of the notes
- take the first competency, and compare evidence given to the behavioural indicators
- write down your evidence on the summary rating form
- refer to the rating scale and rate the candidate on the competency
- repeat the process for the next competency.

A summary rating form

This form sets out the behavioural indicators for each competency, and provides space to record both the evidence and the rating. An example is given at the end of the chapter.

A rating scale

A scale which ties performance against the behavioural indicators to a numerical score (on, say, a nine-point scale) is also required, in order to compare different candidates. An example is again given at the end of the chapter.

SUMMARY

In this chapter, we have described the practical skills needed to undertake competency-based interviews. We have also talked about the process of interviewing, and the various forms required. We further illustrate this process in the case study.

FETTERCORN plc – A CASE STUDY

Ros was keen that the interviews be carried out by the person who would line-manage the new Head Buyer. Before she did any training, however, she wanted some clear guidelines and documentation which had been thoroughly trialled. 'So this is what I will need,' she said. 'Four documents, bound and printed in Fettercorn colours: Fettercorn plc Interviewers' Guidelines, Fettercorn plc Interviewers' Preparation Form, Fettercorn Rating Scale, and Fettercorn Marking Guidelines.'

'There goes the weekend,' thought Jack, but what actually came out of his mouth was 'No problem at all.'

Jack arrived back at the Fettercorn offices first thing Monday morning. He had with him the requested documents, and was prepared to take Ros through them.

'So first we have the interview guidelines. They emphasize the process interviewers should go through. You can reinforce the principles when you do the interviewer training course, but these will also help.'

FETTERCORN plc
INTERVIEWERS' GUIDELINES

- The purpose of this schedule and the interview is to *collect* information on the following competencies:

  — achievement drive
  — influencing
  — interpersonal skills
  — planning and organizing.

- Evidence should be obtained from each candidate on each competency. Plan to spend an equal amount of time per competency, approximately fifteen minutes on each.

- Prepare by reading the candidate's competency-based application form. Choose their best example, and use the question prompts in the Fettercorn plc Interviewers' Preparation Form as a starting point. You may not need to ask all the questions.

- If more evidence is required, ask for an additional example. Evidence can come from in or outside of work.

- Take notes of the candidate's answers so that evidence may be assessed and ratings awarded after the interview.
- Keep in mind that assessment of the candidate takes place after the interview. The interview is for gathering information only.

'Fine. So, what's next?' said Ros. 'Well,' said Jack, 'this is the form that interviewers can use to help them prepare themselves. It has some example prompt questions, although remember that they would not necessarily have to use them all. They are worded in order to elicit evidence relating to the behavioural indicators.'

FETTERCORN plc
INTERVIEWERS' PREPARATION FORM

Achievement drive

Opening question

'In the preparation form, you described a situation where you achieved something difficult. Tell me a little about this . . . '

- Why did you pursue this particular objective?
- Did you face any setbacks? How did you tackle them?
- Was anyone else involved? How did you motivate them?
- What was the outcome?

Repeat these questions for the second example if more evidence is required.

Additional questions

'Could you describe a time when you have tried to accomplish something, but failed?'

- How did the situation arise?
- What did you learn?
- How have you put this into practice?

'Describe a time when you have accomplished a task through effective utilization of others.'

- Who else was involved?

- What was your approach?

- What difficulties did you face? How did you deal with them?

- What was the outcome?

'Very good,' said Ros. 'Now, what about a rating scale? I'm hoping we may be able to use this for the assessment centre exercises as well.' Jack unveiled the rating scale – nine points, anchored at the second, fourth, sixth and eighth. This was his favourite rating scale because of research suggesting that between seven and nine scale points are optimum, and because having even-numbered anchors pushes interviewers away from going 'down the middle'.

FETTERCORN plc
Interview rating scale

Rating	
9	
8 Outstanding	Multiple examples of a high level of competence in this task area. Most (80%) indicators observed in full, with no significant omissions.
7	
6 Good	Clear, unambiguous evidence of competence in this task area. Many indicators (60%) observed in full, and others partially.
5	
4 Development	Some positive evidence, but scope for further development. Some indicators (40%) were fully or partially observed, but other behaviours were omitted.
3	
2 Poor	A few, partially achieved indicators (20%) were observed, but many were absent or were outweighed by negative behaviour.
1	
NE	The interview produced no opportunity to observe this competency.

'And these must be the rating guidelines,' said Ros.

'That's right. As we discussed, they emphasize that rating occurs after the interview has taken place, and that evidence for any competency can come at any point.'

FETTERCORN plc
Marking guidelines

This form should be used *after* the interview to help rate the candidate against the competencies. Evidence relevant to a particular competency could come at any point during the interview so it is important to ensure that all notes are checked against all competencies.

Rating instructions

Start with the first competency and, taking each competency in turn:

- Read through your notes.
- Compare the evidence obtained with the indicators listed in the rating form for the competency.
- On the rating form, where there is evidence of an indicator, place a tick (✓) in the corresponding box.
- When the evidence represents the opposite to an indicator, i.e. a negative behaviour, place a cross (✗) in the corresponding box.
- Where there has been no opportunity to display the indicator, leave the corresponding box blank.
- Write a short summary of the evidence collected for each indicator in the space provided.
- Move on to evidence collected for each of the remaining competencies and repeat the process until all the evidence has been checked against the indicators.
- Rate each competency in turn. Enter this rating in the box for each competency.

'And finally, here is the summary rating form. We'll need to trial them all, of course, but with a little input from line managers, we should end up with a set of practical, useful forms.'

'Well done,' smiled Ros. 'I guess the weekend wasn't a complete waste after all.'

FETTERCORN plc
SUMMARY RATING FORM (sample)

Achievement drive

Indicators

Is proactive at identifying areas in which to add value.

Completes tasks set to time/budget/quality.

Finds ways around problems/setbacks.

Volunteers for extra tasks/duties.

Inspires others to put in extra effort.

Additions:

Evidence/summary

Achievement drive

Oustanding		Good		Development			Poor	
9	8	7	6	5	4	3	2	1 NE – No evidence

Ros flicked through the finished product, a ring-bound booklet containing the interview schedule, the rating scale, the marking guidelines and the summary form. Printed up in Fettercorn colours, she had to admit it looked impressive.

The thing she liked most about it, however, was its simplicity. She had run it by some of the more 'hard-nosed' line managers who at first had grumbled about the amount of paper work and 'form-filling'. However, once their comments and concerns had been taken on board, the final product had been greeted with grudging acceptance – a definite triumph at Fettercorn. She had even trialled it on Jack, who had failed dismally – more evidence that it worked!

Psychometrics and competency-based selection

8

The purpose of this chapter is to discuss whether psychometric instruments – tests and questionnaires – add value to selection processes generally, and then to consider how best to integrate them into competency-based processes. Along the way, various practical issues are addressed, including choice of instruments, integrating psychometric with other evidence, fairness, the possibilities of work sample tests, and feedback.

FETTERCORN plc – A CASE STUDY

Jack's car phone crackled as he drove under a bridge. 'Jack, I can't hear you – you're breaking up . . . ' said Ros.

'I said, so you really want to use psychometrics?' He knew that tests would come up at some point. 'What did you have in mind?'

'Well, numerical and verbal reasoning tests seem pretty standard these days – I wonder whether candidates don't actually expect to sit them when they come for interview. Personality questionnaires I'm less sure about – I've read about the recent tribunal cases, and I want to steer well away from those kinds of problems. I know that selecting to a profile is wrong, but maybe there are other ways to use them.'

Jack was relieved that profiling was off the agenda at least. He pulled off the slip road and on to the M25. 'In terms of personality questionnaires, I think that they can add value to the recruitment process. However, I'd use them at the end as part of the assessment centre – that way you will have time to give full feedback and use them to really explore each candidate's competencies. You'll have to ensure that someone is fully trained, which will add to your resource requirements but, on the whole, there's research to suggest they would be a useful addition.'

'And what about ability tests?' asked Ros. In truth, she was also a little concerned about such tests, in particular the possible adverse impact they might have on women or ethnic minority candidates.

'It all comes down to the job analysis,' replied Jack. 'Your analysis said that numerical and verbal reasoning was particularly important for the job of Head Buyer. That means that you have a good case for including them in your process. My question would be, how will you integrate the information with the other information you are getting on competencies?' He pulled into the Fettercorn car park and spotted a space.

'Can't we just convert the test scores to a score on our nine-point rating scale? We could even just turn them into stanines, couldn't we?'

Jack could see several problems with this approach. He also wanted to run the idea of work sample tests past Ros as a possible alternative. With a resigned sigh he asked 'I've just arrived – can you meet me in reception in a couple of minutes? I just need to call the office, and tell them I may be back a little later than anticipated . . . '

Psychometrics are perhaps what psychologists working in business are most frequently associated with, especially personality assessment. Many of us are keen to understand ourselves further, to confirm something about ourselves we already suspect. The idea that by answering a few questions you might lift the lid on yourself is more or less universally appealing. This has led to a proliferation of pseudo-psychological questionnaires, ranging from those found in popular magazines, which are harmless enough, to those published as *bona fide* occupational tests, which are definitely not harmless. When one psychologist called them 'largely unvalidated quickies'[1], he was being kind. Another psychologist was less kind. Commenting on psychometric instruments generally, he did not mince his words – 'some of the stuff on the market is rubbish. I wouldn't use it to select a toothbrush.'[2]

This bad-mouthing, plus what people experience for themselves, has created doubt and mistrust which has only been fuelled by the well publicised industrial tribunal cases alleging racial discrimination/unfair dismissal as a result of applying psychometrics[3]. You would think that the case for using psychometrics in making selection decisions was decidedly shaky.

If so, the market has not heard. In the EDB survey, as many as 87.3 per cent of the sample use one or more psychometric instruments, and their use has grown markedly since 1991. True, the increase in usage of personality questionnaires for selection has slowed down, which is probably attributable to fallout from those cases. In 1991, personality questionnaires were the most popular of the three selection methods included in the EDB survey; 58 per cent of employers used them, mostly to select managers. In 1996 the figure had stayed more or less the same at 61 per cent. Even so, personality questionnaires are still spreading at the most rapid rate, with 23.6 per cent of users introducing them in the past two years. Incidentally, more than four in five finance sector organizations use personality questionnaires for selection. But then, as we noted before, they use just about everything. Regarding ability tests, the proportion of organizations using them to select at least some groups of staff has risen, from just under 50 per cent in 1991 to around 75 per cent in 1996, making them as popular as, for example, CVs.

The EDB survey attributes the increased use of testing to line managers coming to recognize the predictive validity of tests. Perhaps it is an exercise in self-validation. These managers were among the first to be exposed to tests and perhaps they are taking the view that if they went through them, and have got where they are, then the tests must be sound, and should be used on others.

We have no problems about using tests and questionnaires. The provisos of course are that the instruments used are quality instruments, the purpose of the instruments is clear, and the instruments are used in a way which conforms to best practice standards. When these conditions hold good, utility can be gained from psychometric instruments, whether recruitment and selection is competency-based or not. It would seem that there is a growing belief among personnel and line managers that tests are a prime means of securing more objectivity in selection. In this chapter, we discuss whether that belief is justified.

In what follows, we organize our thoughts along these lines:

- what is psychometrics?
- operational issues around using psychometrics
- integrating psychometrics into competency frameworks, including a treatment of work sample tests
- feedback of results.

WHAT IS PSYCHOMETRICS?

To practise psychometrics is to go about measuring psychological characteristics. 'Psyche' refers to the psychological characteristic, and 'metric' refers to the measurement of it. There is an entire sub-discipline within psychology dedicated to improving the accuracy with which we can measure psychological characteristics, and the various instruments on the market today are the tangible signs of this. The psychological characteristics that HR professionals want to measure most are those related to intelligence, and those related to personality.

It is useful to divide psychometrics into two main categories:

- measures of maximum performance, which indicate what an applicant *can do*

- measures of typical performance, which indicate what an applicant is likely to do, or would *prefer to do*.

Most ability tests (such as numerical, verbal or spatial reasoning tests) fall into the first category, whilst personality questionnaires or inventories fall into the second. It is a matter of regret that ability tests and personality questionnaires are often lumped together – erroneously – as 'psychometric tests'. A personality questionnaire is not a test because there are no right or wrong answers. Ask one of us which of the following we prefer to do: bungee jumping, needlework or collecting for charity, and you get a preference – our preference. It is neither right nor wrong. But ask for the square root of 729 and if the answer is not 27, it is wrong.

Measures of maximum performance

Managers have to take decisions, exercise judgement, solve problems and analyse situations. They have to do other things too, but there is no getting away from the reality that mental power is crucial to successful performance as a manager. Sir James Blyth, now Lord Blyth the chief executive of The Boots Company, believing that complex management jobs require high ability coupled with a personality which is likely to enable high performance in the longer term, introduced psychometric assessment into the company so as to find the best people, whether from outside or inside (personal communication, John Richards and Nicky Hill, 1996). He was right, especially about ability tests. They provide an immediate tap into mental power. All studies agree that tests of general cognitive ability are good predictors of job and training performance when the job or training demands a high level of thought. The more complex the job or the training, the better tests work.

Do ability tests add value to a selection process?

In terms of contributing to good selection decisions, and leaving aside all other considerations, ability tests deliver the biggest bang for the buck, far in excess of personality measures, or interviews, or educational attainments. This does not mean that they are brilliant at prediction – at their best they predict something like 25 per cent of the variance in job performance – but they are the best single measure. And we can almost certainly do better. The tests on the market are without exception tapping into a quite narrow academic ability (the new ABLE series[4] may be different).

There are, of course, many human characteristics which impact on job performance that tests cannot assess, such as getting on with people and showing initiative. An important rider, therefore, is this: ability tests tell us what individuals can do, but they are not good at predicting what they *will* do.

Particularly for applicants with little or no track record, tests provide information which is not readily available elsewhere. But the benefits of testing are conditional on sensible use; they also vary with the nature of the job, the size of the employer, and the resources devoted by the organization to the testing programme. Case law (in the USA) offers ample evidence that tests have at times been so carelessly used as to be irrelevant to the hiring decisions taken, or worse.

Measures of typical performance

Measures of typical performance tell us about our preferences; if faced with a choice between an hour of proof-reading or giving a lecture, which would we prefer to do? They tell us nothing about our ability to carry out these tasks – you may prefer to give a lecture but may be poor at doing so. Nor, if the question is put as a forced choice, which is how *ipsative questionnaires* work, do they tell us anything about whether we would enjoy our choice. Just because we express a preference does not mean that we like doing that thing (would you prefer to climb Everest or K2?).

In his film *Zelig*, Woody Allen tried to show us a man without a personality, when of course there is no such thing. We all have personalities and if we go to work we take them with us. We might leave our brains at the gate (although we shouldn't) but we take our personalities in with us. They then affect how we do the job, and the job in turn affects how we behave. If the upshot is that we behave markedly differently at work compared with outside, then you could say that there is such a thing as an occupational personality.

Two points emerge from this. One is that it is worth trying to get an assessment of personality, simply because it is too important to leave out of the selection equation, and the second is that the assessment should be of behaviour *at work* (see Box 8.1).

BOX 8.1 TRANSPARENCY VERSUS OPACITY

Many of the personality questionnaires available differ in terms of how job related the questions are. At one end of the spectrum are the *transparent* questionnaires, such as the Occupational Personality Questionnaire (OPQ), which contain questions closely (but not exclusively) related to the workplace. This has the advantage that candidates clearly see the value of completing the questionnaire, but the disadvantage that they can easily see what the questions are getting at. At the other end of the spectrum are the *opaque* questionnaires, such as the California Personality Inventory. Here the questions tend to be unrelated to the workplace (there used to be a question, 'Do you prefer taking a bath to a shower?') and it is difficult to see what they are getting at. That means that it is difficult to 'fake good' but also that candidates may take some convincing of the value of completing the questionnaire.

In the UK this has not been a problem – so far – but in California a man successfully brought a case against an employer for requiring him to complete an 'opaque' questionnaire, his grounds being breach of privacy (*Soroka v Dayton Hudson Corp.*, 1993[5]). Having applied to be a security guard for a supermarket chain, he could not understand why he was being asked questions about his sex life.

Opaque questionnaires are rather like biodata (see Chapter 5). They work because they work, and no one knows why. For that reason, it is necessary to spend extra time briefing candidates and explaining the nature of the questionnaire, and how it provides relevant information to help assess job fit.

It might come as a surprise to learn that personality questionnaires differ quite widely in what they purport to measure. On the market you will find questionnaires which claim to measure a range of personality 'dimensions', from 2 to more than 30. Academics and test publishers have been locked in a debate over the 'right' number of scales needed to define personality. Whether the answer is 5 or 25 (see Box 8.2), is a matter of indifference to the user. For the personnel manager using a competency-based system for recruitment, the key question will always be – which questionnaire best taps into the competencies in my framework? This is something we will look at in the next section.

BOX 8.2   THE BIG FIVE AND THE PARSIMONY DEBATE

Personality researchers have arrived at the view that human personality can be described in terms of five basic traits or dimensions, usually called the 'big five'. Naturally, the view is not unanimous – that would be too much to expect from psychologists. The names of the big five are: extraversion, neuroticism (the flip side is emotional stability), openness to experience, agreeableness, and conscientiousness. Note that the words will differ from instrument to instrument.

Most new instruments appearing on the market claim to measure the big five. The publishers of older instruments, like the OPQ, which in its most popular version has 30 scales, argue that five is too few for occupational assessment. What they mean – SHL have said as much – is that more scales provide more detailed descriptions of personality, and therefore more talking points for individual development work. The trouble is that the more scales you throw at people, the less they may understand.

Our view would be that for selection, which is what we are concerned with here, parsimony is what you want; operationally, some agreement on the serious measurement of a small number of scales, call them the big five, or the mega four, or the thunderous three, it really doesn't matter. For a long time Eysenck's two scales – extraversion and neuroticism – were sufficient and some psychologists would say that these are still the only traits which can be reliably measured[7]. They are certainly the only ones which always show up during analysis.

Nearly all instruments which purport to give an assessment of personality rely on the self-report method, where people answer questions about themselves. With self-report it must always be remembered that the data which result are a direct function of what we are prepared to agree to about ourselves (constrained also by our level of self insight). 'Garbage in, garbage out,' as the saying goes. Concrete examples of behaviour are not asked for, nor are we asked, except through repeated questions, to corroborate anything we endorse. The possibility of going beyond self-report is discussed later in the chapter.

Do personality questionnaires add value to a selection process?

Between the 'refuseniks' who dismiss personality measures as worthless, and the academics who argue that personality measures might even be as useful as assessment centres, lies a multiplicity of opinions. For us, the answer to the question must be a guarded 'yes'. It is 'yes' because there is enough evidence that personality questionnaires provide unique predictive power beyond what ability tests can supply. It is guarded because of concerns about what is out there, and how it is being used. Careful academic work does not use 'quickies', but they are a fact of life in the business world. It ought to be obvious that they cannot be expected to capture personality, occupational or otherwise. What is more, they rely on word association, a very dangerous thing to do given the great variation in how we respond to words (think of a word like 'smart' or 'cute'). We would also say that there is a real risk of over-interpretation, of putting people too readily into boxes and of being blind to contra-indications. Above all, far too little is known about the validity of these instruments; the tendency is to let users find out what is useful for them, which is a bit like saying, 'Here are some pills; see what they are good for, and try not to kill anyone.'

We would certainly counsel against using personality instruments in a 'hard' way, such as excluding people because they have a certain profile, or because their scores on specific scales are too low. These instruments are better used towards the end of a recruitment process, perhaps as part of an assessment centre, but always in conjunction with an interview. What the results of a questionnaire can provide is a structure – a set of hypotheses – which can be followed up in an interview which is targeted towards the competencies that are being assessed.

OPERATIONAL ISSUES AROUND USING PSYCHOMETRICS

As well as the validity issue – do psychometrics help to predict future job performance? – there are operational issues to consider when deciding whether or not to use tests and questionnaires. We would single out:

- acceptability
- familiarity
- fairness.

Acceptability

In earlier chapters, we more than once stressed the public relations value of treating candidates with courtesy and respect, and emphasized that recruitment is a two-way street. Accordingly, it is important to understand how candidates experience tests and questionnaires.

Studies comparing the relative acceptability of various selection procedures have generally shown personality questionnaires to be among the least well received[8]. The concerns seem to be centred on invasion of privacy, of which the *Soroka* case (see Box 8.1) is a very good example. But even an obviously job-relevant and inoffensively worded personality measure used in isolation can offend a sizeable number of applicants[9]. The qualifier 'in isolation' is important. It would seem – and this is by no means definitive – that people are more comfortable with personality questionnaires when they are accompanied by face-valid ability tests. It appears that the objectivity and transparency of the latter helps to legitimize the former, especially where it is disguised or opaque. Note that we are talking about relative acceptability. Clearly not everyone is fond of ability tests, as Box 8.3 makes plain. Nor will tests necessarily be preferred over anything else. One study combined tests with a biodata form (see Chapter 5) and found a preference for biodata on the grounds that there was more control over the answers[10].

What these findings suggest – which is very pertinent given the thrust of this book – is that it is the composition of a selection process that affects acceptability perceptions most strongly. Some line-ups appeal more than others. Tests plus questionnaire is a more acceptable combination than interview plus questionnaire, and interview on its own is more acceptable than questionnaire on its own. The message for process designers is to balance up the methods they use. Generally speaking, and as discussed in Chapter 3, a sequence comprised of an application form, an interview, some tests and a questionnaire, and maybe an assessment centre, should find acceptability.

Familiarity

The restricted choice of reasoning tests available to recruiters means that job applicants applying to a number of different organizations may be

---

BOX 8.3   DO I NOT LIKE TESTS!

A 1993 study[11] investigated the experiences of over 700 final year students on the milk round, using questionnaires, focus groups and diaries. Seventy-four per cent (74%) of the students were asked to complete an ability test. When asked what they thought, 40 per cent felt tests were fair, whilst 25 per cent felt they were not. Forty-three per cent (43%) of students answered no to the question 'Are companies that use tests more likely to take selection seriously?'

---

asked to take identical or similar tests on more than one occasion. This gives rise to fears that these candidates may benefit from their prior experience and thus have an unfair advantage over other candidates. The worry is that practice effects will introduce unfairness into the selection process. Obviously, this worry is greatest in the graduate milk round (the study described in Box 8.3 found 40 per cent of graduates had completed the same test on more than one occasion), but it is likely to become much more of a problem as the generation of managers first selected using psychometrics moves up the career ladder.

The problem is that practice tends to make perfect. Studies have shown that if the same test is taken by the same people two weeks apart, some of them will perform significantly better on the second occasion. Richard Hunter and colleagues[12] asked students to complete the SHL numerical and verbal critical reasoning tests twice two weeks apart, and found the differences for some people were quite pronounced. They published some figures for individuals (raw scores and percentiles) which make the point. Table 8.1 has the details.

Evidently, some people increased their scores from as low as the 20th to as high as the 80th percentile when re-tested two weeks later. If there is a minimum score which candidates must reach, then the implications are clear.

The practice effect problem is obviously amplified if, in a group of people being tested (the usual situation in recruitment and selection), some are experienced test takers, and others are not. This is why practice tests, and example questions, are so necessary, along with briefing on how to approach test taking. There are always going to be candidates who, for whatever reason but usually lack of previous exposure to tests, are going to be lacking in 'test wiseness', which means being less adept at all the wrinkles which help to actualize good test performance – smart use of time, attempting all questions, skipping items and returning to them later if there is time, and so on. The so-called 'Paddington Guards' (who were

FIRST OCCASION		SECOND OCCASION	
Verbal	Percentile	Verbal	Percentile
27	10th	34	50th
30	25th	35	50th
33	40th	40	80th
33	40th	38	75th
34	50th	40	80th
35	50th	39	80th
Numerical	Percentile	Numerical	Percentile
14	10th	24	50th
17	20th	30	80th
18	20th	27	70th
20	30th	25	60th
22	40th	28	70th
26	60th	33	90th

Table 8.1   Some Individual Results from Repeated Testing

mostly from the Indian sub-continent, not educated in this country and needing to pass tests in order to become drivers) knew nothing of all this before they received training in test taking[13]. Some of them did not know that, once started, they could turn over pages of the test without being told, or that, if they wanted, they could start at the last question.

Warning candidates beforehand that they will be taking tests is definitely a good thing to do. The EDB survey reports that almost all employers (97.2 per cent) do warn candidates beforehand. Sending out familiarization material and practice booklets ahead of time is also good practice. Familiarity with the tests works to eliminate unwanted sources of error, such as anxiety, which prevent people giving a true account of themselves. So test preparation should actually make the results more valid. But there is a limit to what should be done. Commercial coaching or intensive drilling programmes which teach people how to do particular kinds of questions are to be discouraged since they interfere with validity, and generally damage the credibility of testing.

Less is known concerning practice effects with personality questionnaires. The picture is more complicated because unlike cognitive ability, personality traits are not necessarily expected to remain unchanged. We know that a person's mood and the external pressures on them can affect how they come out on a questionnaire. Whatever the reasons, there is a lack of published test–retest reliability data for modern personality questionnaires. From anecdotal evidence, we can suggest three possible problems resulting from repeatedly taking the same or similar tests. The first is the fatigue effect: 'not another personality questionnaire!', which may manifest in lower test motivation and less insightful answers. The second is the increased likelihood of 'faking good', as candidates become more familiar with the questionnaire's structure. The third we call the 'self-fulfilling prophecy'. Once you have had feedback on your personality questionnaire results, there is the possibility that you internalize this to the extent of saying 'this is my personality', which then influences the way you answer questions in the next personality questionnaire you take. The effect of familiarity on personality questionnaires is an area deserving of more careful investigation.

Fairness

In the UK, employment law makes it unlawful to discriminate at the point of selection on the basis of gender, race, disability and religion (the latter in Northern Ireland). Other EU countries have similar laws, and the USA has civil rights legislation*.

Because tests are objective, neutral and 'blind' it would seem that all test takers would be treated even-handedly. Unfortunately, this does not follow. There are complications which have to be brought into the reckoning. In particular, there are consistently recurring differences between certain groups on certain tests (and questionnaires). For example, on ability tests requiring understanding of written English and where speed of answering is at a premium, ethnic minority candidates in the generality have consistently scored lower – on average – than white candidates[14]. Other ability differences worth knowing about can be found in Box 8.4. It is important to stress, with all these differences, that the overlap in score distributions produced by groups is always considerable. Groups are always much more like each other than not. It is just that at the margin some people could be affected adversely.

There have also been differences reported on personality questionnaires. It had been thought (hoped) that personality questionnaires would not produce results which place any particular group at a disadvantage. Some British work, however, throws doubt on this. A study of the OPQ

---

* It is worth noting that, in UK law at least, a 'test' is defined very broadly to include any instrument used to help make a selection decision. The law thus applies equally to interviews, application forms and assessment centres.

BOX 8.4   GENDER DIFFERENCES IN ABILITIES

From adolescence onwards, there are indications of female superiority in a variety of verbal abilities which continues into adulthood. Spatial ability is an area where males definitely outperform females, especially on tasks requiring three-dimensional rotation of objects. Males also score higher on tests of mechanical reasoning, which of course call on visuo-spatial abilities[15]. Women tend to be better than men at rapidly identifying matching items, a skill called perceptual speed. They have greater verbal fluency, including the ability to find words that begin with a specific letter or meet some other constraint. Women also outperform men in arithmetic calculation and in recalling landmarks from a route. Moreover, women are faster at certain precision manual tasks, such as placing pegs in designated holes on a board[16].

reported significant gender differences on scales such as controlling, persuasive and innovative. Females obtained markedly lower scores, raising the fear that they might lose out simply because males had been more boastful about themselves[17]. Confirmation that there is some cause for concern comes from the validation exercise on the CPI, Firo-B and the MBTI, being carried out by Oxford Psychologists Press, which has thrown up larger gender differences than expected, especially among older and less well-educated groups[18]. A very comprehensive American study found males reporting more assertiveness and slightly higher self-esteem than females. Females, for their part, reported higher than males on extraversion, anxiety, trust, and, especially, tender-mindedness. Gender differences in personality traits were generally constant across ages, educational levels, and nations[19].

So there is a lot to be taken into account when interpreting test and questionnaire results. The reality is that these differences exist, so if you are going to use ability tests, in particular, you should be aware of them and have a strategy for dealing with them. For example, do not use spatial tests or tests of mechanical reasoning unless they are absolutely indicated by the job. Do not use tests which require a lot of written comprehension unless that is absolutely required by the job. In other words, only use a test if the characteristic which it measures can be shown to be vital for effective job performance.

A strategy we would commend is to use test results *conservatively*; to exclude the clearly unsuitable rather than to identify the top performers. Prediction has two aspects, predicting who will be successful and who will not be successful. Ability tests are better at predicting who will not be successful. Generally speaking, bottom-up exclusion will lead to more correct decisions than top-down selection. This is because the highest scorers are artificially, and unavoidably clustered together with no more opportunity to add to their scores.

So you can always say with more confidence that the bottom 20 per cent will fail than that the top 20 per cent will succeed. Even then there will always be some among the low scorers who could do the job well if hired. The principal worry about the fairness of tests has been that these very people (false negatives, if you like) are found disproportionately among traditionally disadvantaged groups like ethnic minorities. It follows (and this is the point of operating the conservative strategy) that the lower the cut-off score, the less likely is disproportionate impact (incidentally, a better term than adverse impact because more neutral).

Evidently, unfairness could be introduced by ill-considered choice of tests or questionnaires, or by uninformed interpretation. Here are some examples of what one of us has called *casual implementation*[20]:

- failing to give adequate notice, or opportunity for preparation, familiarization, and practice

- failing to give feedback, where promised

- failing to explain the relevance of the tests or questionnaires to the job being applied for

- passing results on to others when confidentiality had been promised

- failing to explain how the results will be used

- failing to adapt administration conditions for certain categories of people, e.g. people with disabilities

- continuing to use tests and questionnaires which are known to disadvantage a particular group, e.g. using mechanical reasoning tests with women.

These failings are listed in no particular order of seriousness: they all happen, and they are all avoidable. Sometimes those doing the testing fail to empathize with those on the receiving end, or they don't think, or they don't know themselves how, for instance, results are going to be used. Here we would repeat our position on questionnaires. Do use them but please take the trouble to use them appropriately. Failure to do so can have considerable consequences for the individual, and for the organization.

INTEGRATING PSYCHOMETRICS INTO COMPETENCY FRAMEWORKS

Having discussed in general terms the value of psychometrics in recruitment and selection, we need to look at how (or if) such measures fit in the context of competency-based processes. It is not obvious that the two will integrate; after all, one has been around much longer than the other.

Ability tests

One immediate difficulty is that the information provided, and the information needed, are at different levels, a point made by Clive Fletcher[21]. For example, the competency 'planning and organizing' depends, for its realization, on the expression of several psychological attributes:

Intellect

The ability to see logical relationships; the ability to deduce specifics from generalities, and induce the opposite; the ability to think strategically using 'if . . . then' reasoning.

Personality characteristics

The predisposition to want to plan ahead, as opposed to reacting to situations; methodicalness, conscientiousness and detail-consciousness.

Motivators

A degree of achievement drive.

Ability tests can provide evidence on one, but only one, of these dimensions – intellect. However, this dimension interpenetrates several competencies. Table 8.2 shows how this works for Fettercorn's competency framework.

In this case, a job analysis has identified that competent performance in the area of 'Analysis' requires both numerical and critical reasoning skills, whilst competent performance in the areas of 'Learning ability', 'planning and organizing' and 'Influencing' require critical reasoning skills. This seems reasonable enough; moreover, these skills are relatively simple to

Numerical reasoning	Critical reasoning	Competency
✓	✓	Analysis
	✓	Learning ability
	✓	Planning and organizing
		Achievement drive
	✓	Influencing
		Interpersonal skills

Table 8.2 Ability Tests and Fettercorn's Competency Framework

test. The problems are all in the interpretation. To see this, let us imagine candidates have completed two ability tests – the GMA Numerical and Ravens Advanced Progressive Matrices (an abstract reasoning test).

One particular candidate obtains a score at the 75th percentile on the numerical test, and the 89th percentile on the Ravens (when compared to the appropriate norm group of managers and professionals). This person would appear to possess a high level of reasoning ability, and to be slightly less able (but still very able – well above average) in terms of numerical reasoning. The question now is – how do you relate these scores to the competencies? Should the two tests be given the same weight of importance when arriving at a competency score? Should the tests have the same importance when assigning a competency score to, say, 'Analysis' as to 'Influencing'? Are high scores on the tests necessary and sufficient for a high rating on the 'Analysis' competency, and do low scores mean that you cannot be good at 'Analysis'? And what if you wish to combine the test scores with data from an interview in the screening situation, or with data from other exercises in an assessment centre?

We have tried a variety of ways of transforming test data into competency scores, none of which is perfect. We have arrived at two working solutions. The first is not to integrate the test data into the competency framework at all. Instead, the data are *either* used as separate criteria, perhaps as low cut-off scores, *or* are integrated in a judgemental way (e.g. 'candidate X did well on planning in the in-tray exercise, but produced a low reasoning ability score. This suggests that he or she may have difficulty planning in very complex environments.')

The second solution is to use a banding technique where ranges of ability scores are translated into points on the rating scale. For a competency such as 'Analysis', this is likely to form the lion's share of the final rating. For other competencies such as 'Planning and organizing', a reasonable ability score is likely to be necessary but not sufficient for a high overall competency score. The challenge, of course, is to accurately identify the bands.

Work samples: better suited to competency-based approaches than ability tests

There is an approach to testing which, if not radically different from conventional tests, offers a genuine alternative, and a better way of handling those interpretational problems. It is the work sample test. These are tests which more closely and obviously correspond to the demands of jobs than ability tests. In that respect, they are particularly suited to a competency-based approach. Because of time constraints not every aspect of a job or complex task can be simulated in a work sample. Thus work samples should concentrate only on those competencies which job holders need to possess.

Work sample tests have not been greatly used in this country but the experience to date, here and in the USA[22], is that they are perceived by candidates as fairer, more acceptable and of a more appropriate level of difficulty than conventional ability tests. Also, work sample tests have been shown to produce predictive validities at least as high as conventional ability tests[23].

It is possible to think of a continuum of work sample tests. At one end there are the flight simulators and virtual theatre of war devices used by the military which mirror exactly the conditions of the job. These could be described as *high fidelity* simulations. At the other end of the continuum is something that may look like an ability test, but is not. These could be described as *low fidelity* simulations. The idea is to take a small domain such as making financial decisions, or planning and organizing an event, and produce a set of questions relating to the theme. The tests are then trialled and validated in the same way as an ordinary test. Somewhere in the middle of the continuum are the exercises commonly found in assessment centres, such as in-trays, presentations and group meetings (see Chapter 9).

Between us we have designed paper and pencil work sample tests to measure competencies such as filing accuracy, clerical detail-consciousness, business acumen, problem analysis, decision making, forward thinking, and sensible risk-taking.

Logically, work sample tests should produce less disproportionate impact, precisely because they are matched to the job and extraneous language demands are cut out. That said, the jury is still out. The degree of disproportionate impact is likely to depend on whether the work sample is of the physical kind, requiring a demonstration, or whether it is of the paper and pencil variety. Work sample tests that are paper and pencil and therefore of the same format as ability tests cannot be expected to necessarily eliminate the disproportionate impact often found with ability tests – but they should reduce it.

The main argument against work sample tests is that, as they are usually bespoke tools, they are too costly[24]. This argument can be overdone. While it is correct to say that the initial start-up costs are high, the ongoing costs are negligible. An organization which commissions its own work sample test owns the test. The only costs it bears are around reproducing materials, scoring the tests, and interpreting the results.

To summarize, the strength of the work sample approach is not so much that it is directly relevant to the job in question (because, as we said, jobs may disappear or be re-shaped) but that it obliges test designers to target individual competencies. Jobs may go, but competencies in some form or another will remain, and as such have future human resource value for the organization. As far as we are concerned, work sample tests will always be preferred to ability tests when operationalizing a competency-based selection process.

Personality questionnaires

Just as with ability tests, it is necessary to establish what links exist between specific job competencies and various personality traits. It helps to have worked out ideas about what scales will predict what job behaviours. The best OPQ scale for measuring the competency 'creative/ innovative thinking' appears to be, not surprisingly, 'innovative'. Managers rated high on creativity are able to generate ideas and also have a flair for ingenuity. The 'conceptual' scale also appears to be associated with creativity, suggesting that creative managers are intellectually curious and enjoy dealing with complex and abstract matters[25].

Going back to the Fettercorn competencies (Table 8.2) we can ask what effect introducing some personality measurement will have on the overall assessment. Table 8.3 shows the answer.

Personality measure	Competency
	Analysis
✓	Learning ability
✓	Planning and organizing
✓	Achievement drive
✓	Influencing
✓	Interpersonal skills

Table 8.3 Personality Measures and the Fettercorn Competency Framework

Fettercorn is no different from most competency frameworks in that personality traits have some bearing on nearly all the competencies (except, perhaps 'Analysis'). The difficulty, of course, is identifying where the relationships are, and how seriously to take them. Unless your job analysis has paid attention to personality characteristics (and in our experience most seem not to), then it is left to the 'expert' to hypothesise which scales, and in which combinations, might underlie the different competencies. For example, if Fettercorn decided to use the OPQ concept 5.2, the scales relating to 'influencing' might be:

- persuasive

- controlling

- behavioural

- data rational.

However, it is necessary to look more closely. If people are more 'outgoing' and 'socially confident', they may be more likely to engage in influencing situations; if they are low on 'tough minded', particularly if they are also high on 'caring', they may be less inclined to try to influence others. If they are 'optimistic', then their enthusiasm may help in this regard, and if they are 'critical', they may be more likely to have sorted out their position in advance. Equally, people high on 'competitive/achieving' may have more energy and gusto in such situations.

The point is, we could make a good case for inclusion of almost any of the scales in the OPQ. What is important is not the individual scales, but the overall picture, and no expert system (as yet) can give as much insight as a trained user can in relating that picture to the competency framework. For this reason, we recommend that integration of personality data should occur within the context of a feedback interview focused on the competencies. The result of this should be a rating on each of the competencies. It is then up to the skilled assessor to use the data in the most appropriate way.

There is a basic question raised by all this. If personality questionnaires can be used to pick up on competencies, then why not design a competency questionnaire to do the job? Moreover, one which can be completed by other people. After all, rating need not be restricted to self-report, with all its obvious weaknesses. A mechanism already exists, through reference checks, for seeking others' views about role suitability. The applicant could nominate others from previous work situations (supervisors, colleagues, customers and direct reports) and they could be asked to complete a personality/competency questionnaire. Obviously, asking for preferences would be out of the question since others could not be expected to know what those were. It follows that ipsative measures would be inappropriate, which would be no bad thing.

We already know that others' ratings of competencies or performance characteristics are more accurate than self-ratings[26]. In the workplace, this is likely to be even more the case, for good reasons. Observers come across the individual almost exclusively in the work environment, and so their observations will be strongly, if not wholly, job-related. Individuals, on the other hand, see themselves in numerous situations, such as at home, at play, and at work. The consequence is that observer ratings may be better predictors than self-ratings because there is a much tighter correspondence between the predictor (the rating) and the criterion (job performance)[27]. Not the least virtue of this approach is that it explicitly excludes out of work situations which people, rightly, see as irrelevant to their work behaviour. What is being proposed is not so very different from what is done already in 360 degree evaluation.

FEEDBACK OF TEST RESULTS AND PERSONALITY DATA

Feedback to candidates on how they did on tests and questionnaires is not offered universally – far from it. The EDB survey reports that attitudes to giving feedback are mixed. A high proportion of employers (37.4 per cent) always give feedback to candidates on test performance, but a larger percentage (49.5 per cent) only do so if asked by the candidate. Very few (2.8 per cent) restrict feedback to just the successful candidate, and almost no organizations (1.9 per cent) never provide feedback from tests.

Experience suggests that feeding back test results can wait until the end of the recruitment and selection process. Personality questionnaire results, however, should always be fed back before any selection decision is make. This is because a feedback interview offers an opportunity both to explore the results fully, and to gain further insight into the candidate. We consider feedback in more detail in Chapter 10.

SUMMARY

We have in this chapter outlined the pros and cons of using tests and questionnaires in the context of competency-based recruitment and selection. We have given a guarded 'yes' to the question 'Should they be used at all?', and we have qualified the circumstances in which they should be applied. We have also addressed the question of how to use the results of tests and questionnaires to assess competencies. One particular technique, the work sample test, stands out as being particularly suited to competency-based approaches, and we have explained why this is so.

FETTERCORN plc – A CASE STUDY

'But are you sure they will be ready in time?' demanded Ros, who was not prepared to put her deadline at risk.

'They will be ready – I promise.' Relieved at finally persuading Ros about the value of work samples, Jack resolved to finish analyzing the validation data he had recently collected. The two work sample tests he had developed were nearly complete, and Ros's deadlines gave him enough time to conduct a further trial within Fettercorn itself.

As for personality questionnaires, the pair had decided to use a widely used measure as part of the assessment centre process. A feedback interview would focus on the competencies, and the interviewers would use the personality profile as a structure to guide their probing questions.

Ros stared into her Fettercorn canteen coffee, wondering why if it was so bad, everyone kept drinking it. Market forces clearly did not penetrate this far. All the same, she was pretty content with how the recruitment and selection process was shaping up. With the application form and sifting guidelines in place, the work samples nearly ready, and the interview schedules designed, all that remained was . . .

'Damn, that ruined my brief moment of self-congratulation. We've got an assessment centre to design! It's OK, you can finish your coffee first.' Jack declined the offer.

REFERENCES

1. Ridgeway, C.C. (1995). Understanding the 'person': The need to use alternative assessment methods. *The Occupational Psychologist*, **24**, 17–23.
2. Quoted in: Pickard, J. (1996). The wrong turns to avoid with tests. *People Management*, **8**, August.
3. Wood, R. (1996). Psychometrics should make assessment fairer. *Equal Opportunities Review*, **67**, 27– 33.
4. Oxford Psychologists Press (1996). *The ABLE Series*. Oxford: OPP.
5. Soroka *v.* Dayton Hudson Corp. CalCtAppAo52157 (1993).

6. Saville, P. and Sik, G. (1995). Reductio ad absurdum? *Selection and Development Review*, **11**, 3, 1–3.

   Barrett, P. and Paltiel, L. (1995). *Reductio ad absurdum?* A reply to Saville and Sik (1995). *Selection and Development Review*, **11**, 6, 3–5.

   Saville, P. and Sik, G. (1995). Hitting the target: A rejoinder to Barrett and Paltiel. *Selection and Development Review*, **11**, 6, 6–7.

7. Kline, P. (1994). Advances in occupational personality testing. British Psychological Society Workshop, 'Advances in selection and assessment', 8 July.

8. Rosse, J.G., Miller, J.L. and Stecher, M.D. (1994). A field study of job applicants' reactions to personality and cognitive ability testing. *Journal of Applied Psychology*, **79**, 987–992.

9. Rosse, J.G., Miller, J.L. and Stecher, M.D. (1994). A field study of job applicants' reactions to personality and cognitive ability testing. *Journal of Applied Psychology*, **79**, 987–992.

10. Macan, T.H., Avedon, M.J., Paese, M. and Smith, D.E. (1994). The effects of applicants' reactions to cognitive ability tests and an assessment center. *Personnel Psychology*, **47**, 715–738.

11. Silvester, J. and Brown, A. (1993). Graduate recruitment: testing the impact. *Selection and Development Review*, **9**, 1–3.

12. Hunter, R.A., Keys, A., Wynne, K. and Corcoran, R. (1990). Graduate testing – the problem of practice effects. *Guidance and Assessment Review*, **6**, 5, 1–4.

13. Fletcher, S. and Wood, R. (1996). Enhancing fair selection through access training. *Selection and Development Review*, **12**, 1, 3–5.

14. Schmitt, N. and Noe, R.A. (1986). Personnel selection and equal employment opportunity. In Cooper, C.L. and Robertson, I.T. (Eds) *International Review of Industrial and Organisational Psychology*. Chichester: John Wiley.

15. Gipps, C.V. and Murphy, P. (1994). *A Fair Test: Assessment, Achievement and Equity*. Open University Press, Buckingham.

16. Kimura, D. (1992). Sex differences in the brain. *Scientific American*, September, 81–87.

17. Parker, C. (1994). The OPQ: A closer look at its norms and scales. *Selection and Development Review*, **10**, 4, 2–5.

18. Cook, M. (1997). Gender differences in the CPI. *Occupational Psychology Conference Book of Proceedings*, 77–83.

19. Feingold, A. (1994). Gender differences in personality: A meta-analysis. *Psychological Bulletin*, **116**, 429–456.

20. Wood, R. (1996). Psychometrics should make assessment fairer. *Equal Opportunities Review*, **67**, 27–33.

21. See ref. 13.

22. Robertson, I.T. and Kandola, R.S. (1982). Work sample test: validity, adverse impact and applicant reaction. *Journal of Occupational Psychology*, **55**, 171–183.

23. Robertson, I.T. and Downs, S. (1989). Work sample tests of trainability: a meta-analysis. *Journal of Applied Psychology*, **74**, 402–410.

24. Wood, R. (1994). Work samples should be used more (and will be). *International Journal of Selection and Assessment*, **2**, 166–171.
25. Robertson, I.T. and Kinder, A. (1993). Personality and job competencies: The criterion-related validity of some personality variables. *Journal of Occupational and Organizational Psychology*, **66**, 225–244.
26. Harris, M.H. and Schaubroeck, J. (1988). A meta-analysis of self–supervisor, self–peer, and peer–supervisor ratings. *Personnel Psychology*, **41**, 43–62.
27. Mount, M.K., Barrick, M.R. and Strauss, J.P. (1994). Validity of observer ratings of the Big Five personality factors. *Journal of Applied Psychology*, **79**, 272–280.

Assessment Centres 9

In this chapter, we describe the assessment centre method and why it is partic-ularly well suited to the assessment of competencies as part of a competency-based selection procedure. We offer practical advice on designing and implementing assessment centres, and emphasize the importance of assessor training.

FETTERCORN plc – A CASE STUDY

Ros pulled her chair forward, and launched into her favourite assess-ment centre metaphor.

'OK, Lupita, imagine that you are the manager of a professional hockey team. You need to select a new player. What would you do?'

'I'd send my scouts out to have some players watched, I guess.' Lupita wondered where this was going.

'That's right,' said Ros. 'Maybe even give them a four week trial and see how they perform with your team. Unfortunately, we just can't do that in most cases at work. It's impractical, and there are too many risks – we don't have a reserve team in this business.'

'OK, then I'd hold a trial – I'd invite several players over for a day, and I'd watch them, I'd watch them individually practising skills, and in a couple of practice matches; I'd want to see what they were like when they were on good teams, and when they were really up against it.'

'Excellent,' thought Ros – she was getting somewhere. 'And what would you be looking for?'

'Well it would depend on what position the player was going to have to play. However, in general it would be a combination of different skills – passing, positional sense, tackling, physical strengths, fitness, flexibility, shooting, etc.'

'And would you make the decision on your own?' asked Ros.

'No way – I'd want my specialist coaches to take a look, maybe the captain also.'

'Lupita, you've just described an assessment centre – several candidates, assessed over a day or so by different people, in different situations and conditions, against different criteria. By the way, I didn't know you were a hockey fan.'

'I'm not,' she said. 'I must have read the same assessment book that you have.'

HISTORY

Of all the selection methods, assessment centres lend themselves most easily to the measurement of competencies. This is not accidental, as that is why they were designed in the first place. During the 1939–45 war, psychologists were asked to help select officers to the armed services. Traditional methods, such as the reliance on background and 'breeding', were proving embarrassingly inaccurate, leading to officers being 'returned to unit' due to poor performance in the field[1]. Branches of the British armed services saw a need for a more objective selection procedure based on the requirements of the job in hand. Indeed, a similar approach had already been used in Germany. The idea was that candidates should be faced with tasks or practical exercises which called on them to display the required skills if they had them, and without exposing them to the dangers inherent in the job. Thus, various aspects of the candidate's performance were to be examined from several angles in what amounted to a simulation of what would lie ahead in the job. Obvious, once you think of it.

The approach was picked up by the Office of Strategic Studies, the precursor of the CIA, and also, in the UK, by the Civil Service who began to use it for selecting civil servants. The first commercial application was by AT&T in the USA, around 1954. They used the method to identify potential managers regardless of previous background. AT&T had a place called 'the assessment centre', and it is from here that the name originates. By general consent, it is an awkward term, and really ought to be changed to something like 'selection event'.

ASSESSMENT CENTRE USE IS GROWING

Growth in the use of assessment centres for recruitment and selection has been strong since those early days. A recent survey of 907 organizations employing over 1000 people found that, on average, around 50 per cent of private sector and 39 per cent of public sector organizations used assessment centres, rising to over 60 per cent in some industries, such as food, drink and tobacco; banking, finance and insurance; and police and fire[2]. The survey also found that organizations used assessment centres for a range of applications, such as graduate recruitment, external (non-graduate) recruitment, internal promotion and career development. We would expect the use of assessment centres to expand to include those higher up and lower down organizational hierarchies, where those persist.

WHAT AN ASSESSMENT CENTRE IS

Assessment centres are characterized by multiples. Specifically, there will be multiple:

- candidates

- assessors, or observers

- exercises, simulations or tests

- criteria, or competencies.

An example of a typical assessment centre is one that one of us recently designed for final selection of a call centre manager. Applicants had applied using an application form and, after sifting, those who remained had been further screened using a competency-based interview. Sixteen candidates were invited to attend, eight on the first day and eight on the second. The client provided four assessors who we had previously trained, plus one administrator. The process was run at the client's management training centre.

The assessment centre had been designed to measure eight managerial competencies which fell into the three areas of thinking, relating and acting. To measure them were assembled an in-tray exercise, a role play, a group discussion and a presentation exercise. Tests of numerical and verbal reasoning ability were also included. A matrix showing which competencies were measured by which exercise is shown in Table 9.1.

All competencies were measured by at least two exercises or tests, and no exercise was intended to measure more than five competencies. The tasks requiring interaction with others – the role play, presentation and

	In-tray	Role play	Group discussion	Presenta-tion	Ability tests	Overall
Analysis	✓				✓	
Strategy	✓			✓		
Team work		✓	✓		✓	
Influencing			✓	✓	✓	
Development	✓	✓				
Achievement			✓	✓		
Planning	✓		✓		✓	
Monitoring	✓	✓				

Table 9.1   Exercise by Competency Matrix

group discussion – were observed and marked by assessors, producing a rating of the competencies measured by each exercise. Assessors also marked the in-tray exercise. Each candidate was marked at least once by each of the assessors.

On the day, the candidates completed their work by 2.30 p.m., and were thanked and released. This allowed assessors time to complete their marking, and then discuss each candidate, sharing and challenging each other's observations and ratings. Finally, in a 'wash-up' session, the assessors agreed overall ratings for each candidate on each competency, and made final selection recommendations of 'hire', 'hold' or 'reject', based on previously agreed criteria.

The thing to note about this example, and about all assessment centres, is that, among all the multiples, it is the competencies which hold everything together. The multiple methods and multiple assessors are there to get sound, trustworthy fixes on those competencies. They mean that candidates are seen by different assessors (different perspectives) in different exercises (different situations) and are judged in terms of different attributes (different competencies). You could not implement the assessment centre notion without something like competencies, whatever name you give to them. That is why, unlike tests and questionnaires, assessment centres and competencies fit hand in glove.

Assessment centres offer the best chance of making good selection decisions when the high quality of the remaining candidates requires fine distinctions to be made. That is why they usually appear at the end of a recruitment and selection process. Once you are left with, or have identified, a small number of likely candidates, the assessment centre can provide detailed information on their strengths and development needs, helping you to make an informed decision.

WHAT IS GOOD ABOUT ASSESSMENT CENTRES

The plus points for assessment centres are:

- good validity evidence

- provides a realistic job preview

- favourable candidate reaction

- involvement of line managers

- strategic value.

Validity evidence

Assessment centres have been quite closely studied over the years. One consistent message emerges – well designed assessment centres are the best measures of potential, i.e. the best predictors of future job perform- ance. Notice the qualification in this sentence – 'well designed'. Multiple assessments on their own are not enough if they lack quality and the implementation is sloppy.

A recent meta-analysis[3] – or statistical aggregation of many studies – found that assessment centres measured potential (predicted future per- formance) well. Generally speaking, validities were higher when:

- the percentage of male assessees was low

- a larger number of exercises was used

- assessors were psychologists, not managers

- peer evaluation was used.

Concerning the first, which at first glance looks odd, the explanation may lie in the greater propensity of males to impress at the assessment centre but to fail later on, perhaps through over-promotion relative to females. A related result concerns people from ethnic minorities. For predicting promotion decisions, validities were higher when the percentage of ethnic minorities was low. This could have been because organizations were promoting ethnic minority candidates even though they had low compe- tency scores or, more likely, that they were not promoting them, even though they had high competency scores.

Realistic job preview

As we mentioned in Chapter 4, an important but often overlooked aspect of recruitment is the management of applicants' expectations. We know from research that those with a more realistic expectation of what the job involves show greater commitment, greater job satisfaction and better performance in the long run[4]. The beauty of assessment centres is that, if the exercises are designed correctly, as micro-simulations of the job, then they serve as an excellent realistic job preview. In the assessment centre just described, the in-tray included just the kind of information a call centre manager would be expected to deal with; for example, call rates per hour, call answer times, traffic predictions, team performances, etc. Managers also have to deal with staff who are not performing, so the role play called on candidates to counsel an underperforming member of staff with work and personal problems. Working with other managers to plan the way ahead is something these managers have to do, so the group discussion called on the candidates to plan an overall approach to solving a major staffing problem looming in the near future (i.e. later that morning).

The purpose of the exercises was to provide evidence on specific competencies, but they also provided a realistic preview of what the job would entail. Both of us have been in situations where at the end of the day a candidate has said 'That was fun – but I don't think this job is for me.' We consider that a positive outcome – an expensive mistake was avoided by both parties.

Candidate reaction

Throughout we have emphasized the two-way nature of the recruitment and selection process[5]. Candidates have a choice, too, and we as recruiters must recognize the impact our selection procedures have on their perceptions of us, and on their decisions. The research suggests that assessment centres are regarded by those on the receiving end as a fair and valid way of making a selection decision. Ivan Robertson and colleagues[6] have found that although unsuccessful candidates tend to see assessment centres in a less positive light, *all* candidates tend to see assessment centres in a positive way relative to other selection methods.

Involvement of line managers

When selection decisions are made centrally without input from the person who will eventually manage the appointee, problems can occur. It is clearly vital to get the buy-in of the line manager to any appointment, and to involve him or her in the selection process if at all possible. Assessment centres offer a great opportunity for doing this. Once line managers are trained in the key skills of assessment they can decide on the basis of their observations which candidate to appoint. Any problems that occur later will be a result of their own decision, and so the incentive is there for them to work hard at making the appointment work.

Strategic value

As we said in Chapter 2, competencies have value not least because they provide a way of integrating human resource strategies. Using assessment centres for selection will generate information on individuals which can be plugged into other HR processes. Anyone who is recruited via an assessment centre can be given full feedback on their strengths and development needs expressed in competency terms. This information can then be used to put together a personal development plan, which will feed in to the annual performance review. If the personal development plan becomes a living document and is kept up to date, it has value for career planning and could impact on internal promotion. The assessment centre method fits well within the strategic HR framework.

SOME POSSIBLE FAULT LINES

Some things to watch out for with assessment centres are:

- cost
- over engineering
- skimping on assessor training
- fairness
- what ends up being measured (and not measured).

Cost

There is no doubt that assessment centres are expensive, in anyone's money. They are expensive to develop, they are expensive to run, and they are expensive to maintain. Costs can run into tens of thousands of pounds. The usual counter to this is 'just think how much a poor selection decision could cost you – all those recruitment and salary costs, not to mention any mistakes or poor performance by the person recruited.' This is demonstrably true and cannot be stressed often enough; recruitment mistakes can cost a large proportion of the position's total annual remuneration[7]. An assessment centre will not cost as much as that, even the Rolls-Royce version lasting three days, which is often unnecessary anyway. Getting the right assessors and the right exercises is what matters. There is no point designing the best assessment centre money can buy if you cannot resource it with trained line managers.

Over engineering

On the theme of perfection, designers can work too hard to make simulation exercises perfect. One of the first exercises designed by the second author was so detailed a simulation of a particular job that very few people could complete it. It certainly identified those who could do the job, but was quite de-motivating for those who made very little progress. Again, there is a need for compromise when designing assessment centre exercises: and often the maxim 'the simpler the better' is the one to follow.

Similarly, it is important to be realistic in the overall design of the event. If you know that there is no way you will be able to persuade assessors to spend one day assessing, and one day discussing the candidates (or 'washing up'), then be realistic. Go for a half-day of assessments and a half-day wash-up, starting as early as you can. There is no point trying to squeeze all of the marking and wash-up discussion into a two-hour period late in the evening when everyone is tired. Once someone calls for drinks to be brought in, you know you have gone on too long. Think about this – if you have eight candidates and plan to spend a maximum of 30 minutes discussing each, then that is four hours gone already; and in our experience some candidates will need a lot more discussion than 30 minutes. Realism is the name of the game.

Skimping on assessor training

It is futile designing a great assessment centre if your assessors are not up to scratch. The one thing you should not cut from your budget is assessor training. Better to opt for a one-day assessment centre and a two-day assessor training course, than the other way around. In the untrained state, assessors are awash with hunches, gut feelings, and sometimes just plain prejudice. Anyone who has sat in on a wash-up after the best part of two days of rigorous assessment will know the sinking feeling when assertions are made like 'but he just hasn't got that ... oomph'; 'I know she scored highly on the criteria, but will she fit in?', or 'I know he scored low, but I just have this gut feel that he could go far'.

The effect of poor assessor training is to turn the wash-up into an extended unstructured interview, where assessors look for evidence to confirm or contradict their prejudices and end up selecting people who are similar to themselves. A sure sign that things are really unravelling is when assessors commit the cardinal sin of introducing information about candidates from outside the assessment centre (obviously, this usually only happens with internal candidates). Then it is all about confirming prejudices and equity has gone out of the window, not to mention all of the money spent on the centre. We will have more to say about assessor training later in the chapter.

Fairness

The assessment centre survey quoted earlier asked several questions around equal opportunities issues in the design, development and running of assessment centres. The results can be found in Box 9.1. It is likely, said the report, that organizations do not actually know whether adverse impact or unfair discrimination is actually occurring within their assessment and development centres, and warned employers against 'blind faith' in such centres. Three years on, we would say the same. Powerful tool it may be, but the assessment centre is not exempt from the scrutiny given to other methods.

What ends up being measured (and not measured)

Going back to Table 9.1, it is obvious that if each exercise is measuring the appropriate competencies accurately, we would expect a person's scores on 'Influence', say, to be similar across the three exercises, scores on 'Strategic' to be similar across two exercises, and so on. What we would not necessarily expect would be for scores on different competencies within the in-trap, or within the interview, to be similar.

That is what we would expect: this is what research findings say typically happens:

- ratings of competencies within exercises are highly related

- ratings of competencies across exercises are weakly related.

We are talking here about the so-called exercise effect[8]. The suggestion is that assessors are rating overall performance on each exercise rather than

---

BOX 9.1   EQUAL OPPORTUNITIES AND ASSESSMENT CENTRES

The assessment centre survey found that only:

- 13% of organizations examined the results of the job analysis for bias;
- 27% reviewed competency definitions for stereotyped bias;
- 28% reported reviewing the appropriateness of exercise content for under-represented groups; and
- 36% covered equal opportunity issues in assessor training.

In addition, almost half of the organizations did not carry out systematic monitoring of the 'pass rate' for women and ethnic minority candidates; and almost 80% omitted to analyze the performance of women, ethnic minority and disabled candidates.

---

distinguishing between the competencies. This is an important finding. If assessors are just making global judgements there is room for subjective bias which negates the whole purpose of the assessment centre.

Reducing the exercise effect would increase the validity of assessment exercises, and as such it is a useful goal. One of us, with two colleagues, has summarized the suggestions made over the years to reduce the exercise effect[9]. These included:

- ensuring exercises reflect the target job

- ensuring exercises and competencies are well matched

- reducing the information load on assessors through
  - thorough training
  - using behavioural checklists so that assessors produce ratings through scores
  - using a small number of well-defined competencies
  - mixing palpably different competencies in each exercise, e.g. helicoptering and detail-consciousness, so as to break down 'halo' and 'horns' effects.

These are all good suggestions but the exercise effect has been around for so long that we are tempted to call it structural. The situation is complicated by the fact that what it connotes can be naturally occurring. This will happen when measures of certain competencies happen to be highly intercorrelated within a group of persons. If, for whatever reason, people who are high on 'Empathy' also happen to be high on 'Learning orientation', there is nothing you can do about it. Similarly, if the behaviours required for 'Communication' are also important for effective 'Influencing', then you should expect those competencies to be correlated.

THE KEY STAGES IN THE DESIGN OF AN ASSESSMENT CENTRE

In practical terms, there are *nine* stages to consider when designing an assessment centre. They are:

- identify the competencies you wish to measure
- identify and work within practical constraints
- identify or design exercises and other measures
- arrive at a decision rule
- attend to the logistics, especially the timetable
- communicate with internal stakeholders
- brief candidates
- train assessors
- monitor and evaluate the centre.

We will not go into too much detail on each of these points; there are several standard textbooks available about assessment centres. We will try instead to summarize the practical considerations.

Identify the competencies you wish to measure

These must come from a job analysis or competency-elicitation study. If you are using assessment centres as the final part of a competency-based recruitment and selection process, then you will already know which competencies you have to choose from. Depending on how many competencies there are, and the likely duration of the assessment centre, you may choose to concentrate on measuring a sub-set of key competencies – perhaps the ones which job analysis revealed to be the most important, the ones which have not been measured well in previous parts of the selection process, or competencies which lend themselves particularly well to the assessment centre process, such as team work and persuasion. We have developed assessment centres to measure as few as four competencies, and as many as twelve. Our experience suggests that around eight or nine is the optimum number for practical purposes, although research[10] suggests that less may be more technically realistic. The magic number seven tends to be mentioned.

Identify and work within practical constraints

This is an issue we have already alluded to. If you are designing an assessment centre for recruiting graduates into foreign exchange trading roles, and you know that there is no way established traders would take more than one day away from their desks to act as assessors, then you must take that constraint on board and design your assessment centre around it. Although there may be a point at which shrinking the centre further would compromise its validity, we cannot stress enough the need to be realistic when designing assessment centres.

Identify or design exercises or other measures

How do we know which exercises are best at measuring particular competencies? In fact, there is substantial research here to provide guidelines. Some data from an early study by Byham and Thornton[11] was updated by the second author to include more modern competencies such as 'customer focus'. The table shows which competencies tend to be observed most often with different exercise types. A section of the table is reproduced below as Table 9.2[12].

Once you know which type of exercise you need, there are three options open:

- buy an off-the-shelf exercise

- customize an off-the-shelf exercise

- design your own bespoke exercise.

Off-the-shelf exercises have the advantage that they are usually well produced and well tested. The disadvantage is that they are usually generic, i.e. they are unlikely to reflect accurately the job being recruited for. They are also unlikely to reflect the organization's culture, and these two points together mean that they will not function as a truly realistic job preview.

For those in the graduate recruitment market, there is the added problem of candidate familiarity with particular exercises, not to mention licence fees for repeat use.

Bespoke exercises also have down sides. Designing exercises is quite an art, and there is precious little published that will help. As part of a collaborative research project, we and our colleagues have devised a model of exercise design, and some practical tools to support that process. A summary of the model is shown in Figure 9.1 and is described more fully elsewhere[13].

Other problems associated with bespoke exercises are the initial costs, which include investigation, design, piloting and validation. Once these costs are met, however, there are no ongoing licence fees. The advantages of bespoke exercises are the obvious ones. They can be completely tailored to the job so that the language, issues and nature of the exercises can all reflect the organization's culture. Together, these points mean that the exercises are likely to function as a valid realistic job preview.

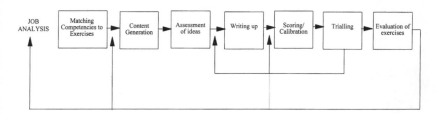

Figure 9.1 Exercise Design – the Practitioner's Model

Arrive at a decision rule

At this point, a key decision must be made – what pattern of results will indicate a successful candidate? We shall discuss this issue more fully in the next chapter, but it is important that the decision rule is agreed before the assessment centre runs. Again, reference will need to be made to the job analysis, but a typical decision rule looks like this:

Successful candidates must score at least a six (on a nine-point scale) on

- team working
- achievement drive

	Business game	In-tray and de-brief	Group discussion (assigned)	Group discussion (non-assigned)	Case study	Scheduling	Interview	Fact-finding	Role play	Oral presentation
Time to mark (mins):										
One competency	15	20	15	15	20	10	10	10	15	10
Whole exercise	45	60	45	45	60	30	40	40	45	45
COMPETENCIES										
ACHIEVEMENT										
Initiative/proactivity	✓✓	✓✓	✓✓	✓✓					✓	
• does not wait to be told what to do										
• instigates action to achieve objectives										
Work standards		✓✓		✓✓	✓		✓✓			
• identifies better ways of doing things										
• regularly meets standards set										
Planning and organizing	✓✓	✓✓			✓	✓✓	✓✓			
• develops detailed action plans										
• determines priorities for tasks										

Table 9.2

	Business game	In-tray and de-brief	Group discussion (assigned)	Group discussion (non-assigned)	Case study	Scheduling	Interview	Fact-finding	Role play	Oral presentation
Tenacity • perseveres when progress blocked • follows issues through to conclusion			✓✓				✓✓	✓✓	✓	
Independence • stands up for own decisions • takes responsibility for results		✓✓					✓✓	✓	✓	
Adaptability • thinks on feet during discussions with staff • understands the need for change	✓✓						✓			

KEY

✓✓ = Competency observed over 90% of the time
✓ = Competency observed over 90% of the time in certain exercises in this category, but not all

Table 9.2 *continued*

and at least a five on all other competencies.

Fixing the rule in advance avoids the potential for any 'foul play'. The rule may have to be revised if too few or too many candidates are subsequently 'successful', and again the important point is that the rule must be applied equally to all candidates. We consider decision making more fully in Chapter 10.

Attend to the logistics, especially the timetable

We have heard assessment centres referred to as a 'logistical nightmare', only to be called a 'dream' when they come off. To mitigate the horror, it is recommended that one person takes responsibility for all of the organization, which usually means booking hotel rooms and training rooms, arranging for materials to be photocopied, sending out briefing documents, and organizing food and refreshments. None of this can happen without reference to the bane of every assessment centre designer's life – the timetable.

Timetables are a headache because there are so many simultaneous constraints to be satisfied. To make best use of time, candidates will be working on different exercises at the same time. Assessors must be rotated so that they see all of the candidates during the day. Assessors need time during the day to mark exercises. Some assessors may not want to interview particular candidates if they already know them well. On top of that, you may only have three rooms to work with.

Unfortunately, we can offer no magic bullet here. We have found no substitute for the pain of timetable design (except to ask our colleague Sean Boyle to do it). Individual timetables for candidates and for assessors are a good idea, so that confusion over who should be where and at what time is minimized.

Communicate

It is important that all the players understand the purpose of the assessment centre, its nature, and what will happen after the centre. There are three key groups of players:

- external candidates

- internal candidates

- other internal stakeholders.

External candidates

External candidates must be thoroughly briefed in advance. This briefing should include a short description of the event (how long it will last, what exercises they will be completing), travel and accommodation arrangements, and a request to inform the company if candidates have any special requirements.

Internal candidates

Internal candidates will require the same briefing, but in addition will need further reassurances about who will see the information from the centre, what will happen if they are/are not successful, etc.

Other internal stakeholders

Other internal stakeholders might include functional budget holders, line managers, and senior HR people. Their commitment and buy-in must be obtained if the assessment centre is to be a success.

Train assessors

As we have said, to skimp on assessor training is certainly a false economy. But it happens, and it bothers people. You may be surprised to know that in the survey of assessment centre practice previously referred to, assessor training emerged as the concern most often mentioned[14]. Apart from calling for more and improved training, a common theme was the notion of training to a standard. Respondents would have been well aware that while at least one assessor must be trained and certified in the interpretation of tests and questionnaires where those are used on assessment centres, for assessing on the centre as a whole there is no such requirement. Box 9.3 has the results in detail.

That employers might act against poor assessors is at least a little reassuring but overall there are no grounds for complacency at all. It is not as if licensing of assessors for assessment centres would be difficult to arrange: a parallel would be the advanced driving test as opposed to the ordinary driving test. Assessors in other walks of life need to be accredited before they can practise. It needs a professional body to start the ball rolling.

For a flavour of what thorough training is like, Box 9.4 contains the training objectives set out in the US guidelines for assessor training[15].

BOX 9.3   WHAT EMPLOYERS SAY ABOUT ASSESSOR TRAINING

Of the 75 organizations which replied to the survey, only 12% said that trainee assessors were assessed against defined standards or criteria, compared with 44% who said that no formal evaluation is made. To the question, 'Must trainees be certified/authorized before acting as assessors?', 47% said 'yes' and 45% said 'no'. However, when asked what form that certification might take, only 11% said that assessors must pass training, 7% said that assessors must practise under supervision after training, while 8% said that assessors must be certified by an external agency or consultant. As to the circumstances under which certification could lapse or be withdrawn, the most commonly given reason was 'poor standard of assessors'.

Assessor training should normally take between two and five days, depending upon level of experience, and the number of exercises used in the centre. We favour a kind of 'just-in-time' training, perhaps running the training and the centre back-to-back, so that assessors do not have time to forget what they have just learned.

Monitor and evaluate the centre

Once the assessment centre is up and running, results need to be monitored, and the success of the centre evaluated. The assessment centres survey previously cited told us that few organizations have validated their centres. Sometimes there is a reason for this. Organizations may feel that in twelve months' time, the competencies they are looking for will have changed, and so there is little point in trying to validate the current centre, even if the time were available. Even so, they still have the problem of wondering whether they can trust the results now. In Chapter 10 we consider some constructive ways of thinking about validation.

SUMMARY

We have described assessment centres, and their suitability for measuring competencies, which is considerable since they were meant to do that from the beginning. We have identified their 'pros' and 'cons', and outlined

BOX 9.4 ASSESSOR TRAINING OBJECTIVES

Competent assessors must display:

- Thorough knowledge and understanding of the assessment methods, relevant dimensions to be observed, expected or typical behaviours, examples or samples of actual behaviours, and so on.
- Thorough knowledge and understanding of the assessment dimensions (competencies), their relationship to job performance, examples of effective and ineffective performance, and so on.
- Demonstrated ability to record and classify behaviour in dimensions, including knowledge of forms used by the centre.
- Thorough knowledge and understanding of evaluation and rating procedures, including how data are integrated by the assessment centre staff.
- Thorough knowledge and understanding of assessment policies and practices of the organization, including restrictions on how assessment data are to be used.
- Thorough knowledge and understanding of feedback procedures where appropriate.
- Demonstrated ability to give accurate oral and written feedback, when feedback is given by the assessors.
- Demonstrated knowledge and ability to play objectively and consistently the role called for in interactive exercises, for example, one-on-one simulations or fact-finding exercises, when this is required of assessors.

some of the practical steps to take when using assessment centres as part of a competency-based recruitment and selection process. We have not yet discussed in detail how to make final selection decisions using the evidence from the assessment centre or, where there is not an assessment centre in the process, from the other evidence gathered. That is what we will do in the next and final chapter.

FETTERCORN plc – A CASE STUDY

After yet another long and tortuous week, Jack and Ros had between them designed an assessment centre for the final stage of the Head Buyer recruitment process. After sounding out the senior management team, who had agreed to act as assessors, Ros had settled on a one-day assessment centre. The centre was to consist of:

- a written case study where the candidate had to analyze information relating to the global supplier base of an imaginary company not unlike Fettercorn

- a presentation, with recommendations, based on the case study

- a role play with a potential supplier, again following on from the information given in the case study

- a personality questionnaire and feedback interview

- an interview which picked up on two competencies and provided an opportunity for information exchange.

The assessment matrix is shown as Table 9.3.

	Case study	Presentation	Role-play	Interview	Personality question-naire
Analysis	✓		✓		
Learning ability	✓			✓	✓
Influencing		✓	✓		✓
Interpersonal skills		✓	✓		✓
Planning and organizing	✓			✓	✓
Achievement drive		✓	✓		✓

Table 9.3 Assessment Matrix for the Fettercorn Assessment Centre

'The assessor training is all set up – two days in all, half a day on each exercise and half a day on the overall process and the wash-up. We've invited volunteers in to act as candidates, and we'll be video-taping the assessors to help them see the errors of their ways.'

Lupita was happy with the assessment centre design. Even the timetable, done without the help of Sean Boyle, looked watertight. 'What about the personality questionnaire, though – don't you need to be trained to use it?' 'That's right,' said Jack.

'No problem,' said Ros, 'I'm trained. Why don't I feed back to the candidates, and then input my findings at the wash-up? That way you and the rest of the management team will have more time for marking.'

'The date is set, and candidates have been invited.' Jack had spotted what was coming next.

'So Jack, how is this wash-up going to work, then?' asked Lupita.

REFERENCES

1. Ballantyne, I. and Povah, N. (1995). *Assessment and Development Centres*. Aldershot: Gower.
2. Boyle, S., Fullerton, J. and Yapp, M. (1993). The rise of the assessment centre: a survey of AC usage in the UK. *Selection and Development Review*, 9, 1–4.
3. Gaugler, R.B., Rosenthal, D.B., Thornton, G.C. and Bentsons, C. (1987). Meta-analysis of assessment center validity. *Journal of Applied Psychology*, 72, 493–511.
   Hunter, J.E. and Hunter, R.F. (1984). Validity and utility of alternative predictors of job performance. *Psychological Bulletin*, 96, 72–98.
4. Premack, S.Z. and Wanous, J.P. (1985). A meta-analysis of realistic job preview experiments. *Journal of Applied Psychology*, 70, 706–719.
5. Herriot, P. (1988). Selection as a social process. In Smith, M. and Robertson, I.T. (Eds) *Advances in Selection and Assessment*. Chichester: Wiley.
6. Robertson, I., Iles, P., Gratton, L. and Sharpley, D. (1991). The impact of personnel selection and assessment methods on candidates. *Human Relations*, 44 (9), 963–981.
7. Smith, M. and Robertson, I.T. (1993). *The Theory and Practice of Systematic Personnel Selection* (2nd Edition). London: Macmillan.
8. Robertson, I.T., Gratton, L. and Sharpley, D. (1987). The psychometric properties and design of managerial assessment centres: Dimensions into exercises won't go. *Journal of Occupational Psychology*, 60, 187–195.
   Sackett, P.R. and Dreher, G.F. (1982). Constructs and assessment center dimen-

sions: Some troublesome empirical findings. *Journal of Applied Psychology*, **67**, 401–410.

9. Ahmed, Y., Payne, T. and Whiddett, S. A process for assessment centre design: A model of best practice. *International Journal of Selection and Assessment*, **5**, 62–68.

10. Gaugler, B.B. and Thornton, G.C. (1989). Number of assessment center dimensions as a determinant of assessor accuracy. *Journal of Applied Psychology*, **74**, 611–618.

11. Thornton, G.C. and Byham, R.N. (1982). *Assessment Centres and Managerial Performance*. New York: Academic Press.

12. Whiddett, S. (1996). *Tools for Designing Assessment and Development Centres*. London: Institute of Personnel and Development.

13. Whiddett, S. (1996). *Tools for designing assessment and development centres*. London: Institute of Personnel and Development.

14. Wood, R. (1996). Assessor training for assessment centres. *Training Officer*, **32**, 55–56.

15. Task Force on Assessment Center Guidelines (1989). Guidelines and Ethical Considerations for Assessment Center Operations. *Public Personnel Management*, **18**, 457–470.

Decision making and evaluation

10

In this, the final chapter, we deal with the end product of a recruitment and selection process – the selection decision. We examine the reasons why decision making is difficult, and compare human decision making with statistical, or equation-driven, decisions. We move on to consider various decision making processes, with particular reference to assessment centres. There follows a short selection on giving feedback, and we finish with advice on evaluating and monitoring the process as a whole.

FETTERCORN plc – A CASE STUDY

Ros was dead on her feet. The other assessors had at least experienced some variation during the day. She, though, had just completed six consecutive personality questionnaire feedback sessions – a cruel and unusual punishment. Looking round she saw Jack nattering to the administrator. 'Why did I invite him today anyway?' she thought. Still, at least she had written up all her notes and was ready for the 'wash-up', as Jack called it.

In the main room the assessors were frantically concluding their marking before the 3.00 p.m. deadline. As Ros walked in she was greeted by a cacophony of pantomime boos and hisses.

'Okay, okay, it's nearly all over. I know you've enjoyed it really. Think, you could have been working!'

As the assessors shuffled their papers. Jack sidled up to the front of the room and turned on the overhead projector. 'Which candidate would we like to consider first?' he smiled.

'We?' thought Ros. 'Cheek.'

'I reckon that there are three we can chuck out straight away,' said Sam, one of the more vocal assessors.

'Hang on,' said Jack hurriedly. 'We have a process here, and we should stick to it. How about looking at the scores on the doors ...'

DECISIONS, DECISIONS . . .

Elaborate selection methods – tests, interviews or assessment centres – will not make the final selection decision for you. Instead, what such methods *can* do is provide information to aid your decision. But what do you do with the information (or evidence) that your competency-based recruitment and selection process produces? How do you use it to make the right decision? It seems to us that there are three cardinal rules when it comes to decision making:

- have a clear set of decision criteria
- apply them equally to all candidates
- make sure that the people making the decisions are trained.

The first two rules are obvious, perhaps too obvious, and for that reason are not always followed. What may appear to be clear criteria at the outset can have a nasty habit of unravelling once real candidates are on the scene. The third rule is less obvious, and so again is likely to be overlooked. It is, of course, vital, and all three rules should be addressed during assessor training. There is also a fourth rule, which is:

- gather as much evidence as you can, within practical constraints.

Anyone who has to make a big decision – a farmer deciding when to cut the corn, an investor trying to work out when to sell – tries to gather information which will help them come to the best decision. The information could be a weather forecast, or the price of some shares they have been tracking. Whatever it is, the information is sought in order to reduce risk.

Selection of people is no different. Because it is an inexact science, the methods we have discussed throughout the book – tests, questionnaires, interviews and assessment centres – serve the necessary purpose of reducing risk. Specifically, these methods help to minimize the risk of selecting a really inappropriate person, and maximize the probability of selecting the right person(s). As we noted in Chapter 7, it is probably easier to accomplish the first objective than the second. That said, there are obvious examples where decision making processes are poor. In Chapter 3 we mentioned that British Members of Parliament are typically selected by what amounts to a mass vote on their presentational skills. That does not seem to us a method likely to minimize the chance of letting through a rogue, and it obviously does not. Of course, the decision makers are not trained, nor could they be, but that begs other questions, like why cling on to such an obviously flawed selection method?

Throughout Chapters 4 to 8 we have been concerned, sometimes implicitly, with the making of decisions. Every time you sift out candidates, you are making decisions. In the next section, we concentrate on the final decision – the appointment. Whereas the earlier decisions were concerned with predicting who would *not* perform well in the role, this final decision is more difficult; how to predict who will do well in the role. To arrive at a decision-making process will itself require decisions:

- the first decision – based on single or multiple sources of evidence?

- the second decision – made by people or equations?

- the third decision – using combined or separate evidence?

THE FIRST DECISION – BASED ON SINGLE OR MULTIPLE SOURCES OF EVIDENCE?

Making a decision based on a one-shot assessment – a single test score, for example – is definitely not recommended, for all the reasons given in this book. A certain soccer manager in the UK is reputed to have bought a striker solely on the basis of having seen a video of his goals – not a good idea – and it hasn't worked out. If the single measure happens to be an ability test, then the chances of producing disproportionate impact on one group or another using top-down selection are considerable. When the Inns of Court School of Law were selecting people to train as barristers (Chapter 3), they used, in the first year (only), the Watson-Glaser critical reasoning test. Happily, they did not make decisions based on the Watson-Glaser alone, but consider what might have happened if they had. With a maximum score of 80 on the test, as many as 570 of 2243 applicants, or 25 per cent, scored 70 or more Out of the 100 top scoring applicants, 98 were men. Whereas 30 per cent of male applicants scored 70 or more, for female applicants the figure was 18 per cent. Of these only 5 per cent were ethnic minority applicants. Looking at who scored 55 or less, the figure for males was 14 per cent, for females 20 per cent, but for ethnic minorities 50 per cent. Quite why the figures should turn out like this is a story in itself[1], but the example does illustrate the perils of making a decision on one measure only. In this case, when other measures were added in, the adverse impact was mitigated considerably.

In a competency-based recruitment and selection process, it would be extremely unlikely for evidence to come from a single source. Indeed, there should be evidence for each candidate on each competency, which automatically generates several pieces of information. As our fourth rule

stated, the more evidence you can collect relating to a candidate's competence, the better. The question then becomes, 'So what do I do with all of
this evidence? How do I integrate it?'

THE SECOND DECISION – MADE BY PEOPLE OR EQUATIONS?

Ostensibly, there are two ways to integrate evidence – either you study the
numbers and come to a decision, or you plug them into an equation and let
it produce an answer. Which do we think would do best – your head or an
equation? It may surprise – and shock – you to know that it is the latter.
The equation is best. In virtually every one of the 100 or so comparative
studies in the social sciences, the statistical method (prediction by equations) has equalled or surpassed the clinical method (prediction by
combining the information in your head), sometimes slightly and sometimes substantially[2]. This means that statistical (linear) models of how
people make decisions have done a better job than the people themselves.
In other words, if someone took the trouble to model how any one of us
makes decisions, and applied that model every time a decision needs to be
made, there will be more good decisions and fewer poor decisions than the
decisions we would make ourselves. Consistent behaviour does best, but
we get bored with that and seek to ring the changes – a bad move.

Making your mind up

Why are we so poor, on the whole, at making decisions? Or rather, why
are we so poor at making decisions about other people? If we had to point
to one root cause, it is that people have difficulty handling a lot of
information. Imagine an assessment centre which measures six competencies on a nine-point scale. That gives – well, a lot of possible profiles.
Add to that the number of candidates, and the demanding nature of an
assessment centre, and it becomes a surprise that we can even decide
which candidate is which.

Information overload is a real problem for human beings, and we have
devised many ways to cope, that is, to simplify the information coming
our way. While this may help us to survive in the jungle, it does not help
us make objective decisions about people. Some of the obstacles to effective integration of information (and subsequent decision making) are
shown in Box 10.1.

Of these impediments to sound judgement, the process of generalizing,
or stereotyping without examining our assumptions, is perhaps central.

BOX 10.1   BARRIERS TO INFORMATION PROCESSING

There are many potential barriers to effective information processing. Some examples which are particularly relevant to selection decisions are given below:

- *Lack of concentration*; tiredness, boredom or lack of motivation can lead to poor levels of concentration.
- *Stereotypes*; mental shortcuts which help us simplify the world can cause us to prejudge in the absence of evidence, or operate as self-fulfilling prophecies.
- *Prejudice*; an extreme case of stereotyping which will lead to a negative evaluation of a person in most cases, regardless of information available.
- *The 'halo' and 'horns' effect*; when an overall evaluation of someone is made – positive or negative – then this can influence all subsequent judgements.
- *The primacy and recency effect*; evidence brought out early in the process or towards the end of the process which is weighted out of proportion.
- *Inaccurate causal attributions*; the way we attribute the causes of events is prone to error. For example, if we fail then it is the situation – if others fail it is their fault.

Recent research into mistakes at work[3] points to generalizations and untested assumptions as major causal factors. Military chiefs are particularly prone to getting it wrong in this way, whether it is Napoleon and Hitler invading Russia, or Haig on the Western Front. How is it that at the Battle of the Somme in 1916 the British High Command, having presumably surveyed the terrain (open *and* uphill), taken cognizance of the weather (very hot), and noted the weight of what the men had to carry (very heavy and cumbersome), nevertheless decided it was a good idea to send the infantry over the top? Because they assumed, or wanted to believe, that the artillery barrage had knocked out the enemy defences.

Equations to the rescue?

Equations are not subject to the information processing difficulties that we are. Like the software devised to sift CVs discussed in Chapter 5 they are, happily, blind to stereotyping, prejudice or 'gut feel'. Unless asked to do so, they will not produce comments like, 'But will she fit in on the shop floor?' Equations use whatever evidence you give them – no more, no less – and, unlike people, equations are always consistent.

Now, we are not computer nerds, and we recognize very well the objections to the use of equations for making selection decisions. As we said in Chapter 6, one of the reasons that interviews are ubiquitous is that recruiters want to meet the candidate face-to-face, and vice-versa, as this gives them both an opportunity to exercise their judgement. Similarly, one of the benefits of using line managers as assessors at an assessment centre is to get their involvement and buy-in to the subsequent appointment(s). Imagine how they would react if, after providing their competency ratings, they were to be told, 'Thanks very much – we'll just feed these scores into the computer and let you know who to appoint.'

The second problem with statistical decision making is that you somehow have to construct an equation which combines all of the evidence you have. In an assessment centre, this could mean combining the different competency ratings in a way which reflects their relative importance and predicts future job performance. A typical equation might look something like this:

$$\text{Final score} = (2.1 \times \text{Competency 1}) + (1.3 \times \text{Competency 2}) \text{ etc.}$$

The numbers are called weights, and reflect the relative importance of the competency when predicting future performance. They are usually arrived at through a validation study which looks at the statistical relationship between each competency and some measure of future job performance. For this, you need to have been running your assessment centre for some time, and to have assessed several hundred candidates.

Summary

The research strongly suggests that equations are as good, if not better, at predicting which people will perform well in the job in future. They are also cheaper. However, there are 'political' difficulties around acceptability, not least the almost certain loss of line manager involvement in the decision.

THE THIRD DECISION – USING COMBINED OR SEPARATE EVIDENCE?

When faced with multiple sources of evidence – for example seven overall competency ratings from an assessment centre, or a battery of test scores – there are two options: examine the information as it stands and refrain from aggregating it, or combine the scores or ratings into a single number. This may be done as previously discussed through a complex equation, or more simply by adding up or averaging the scores in a weighted or unweighted way. To make this clearer, we would like to illustrate the possible decision processes that could be used in an assessment centre. At assessment centres, the pooling and integration of evidence from assessors is at the heart of the process. There are three potential steps:

- discuss the evidence and agree a rating for each 'cell'
- combine the evidence for each competency into an overall competency rating
- make the decision, either through combination or separation.

Discuss the evidence and agree a rating for each cell

It may help at this point to refer back to Table 9.1 – the exercises by competencies matrix. This matrix consists of a series of 'cells', one for each time a competency is measured in an exercise. In the survey of assessment centre usage cited in Chapter 9[4], three possible scenarios for the treatment of each individual cell of the matrix were presented to respondents who were asked to indicate which came closest to their own procedure:

1. *Assessor reports evidence and rating.* The observing assessor reports evidence together with a rating. Other assessors then discuss the evidence and agree or amend the rating.

2. *Assessor reports evidence – group agrees rating.* The observing assessor reports evidence only – no rating is given. With other assessors, they then discuss the evidence and the group jointly agrees a rating.

3. *Assessor reports evidence – other assessors individually assign ratings, then agree.* The observing assessor reports evidence only – no rating is given. Each assessor then individually assigns a rating on the basis of the evidence presented. The individual ratings are then announced and discussed. A single rating is then assigned by agreement or by averaging.

Table 10.1 shows the results. Clearly the most common approach is for assessors to report their evidence and ratings before any discussion takes

	% (N = 64)
Assessor reports evidence and rating – group agree rating	60
Assessor reports evidence – group agree rating	19
Assessor reports evidence – others individually assign ratings, then agree	19
Other method	2

Table 10.1   How Assessors and the Group Interact in the Wash-up[1]

place. This is a pity. Assessors are more likely to accept a rating without challenging it when it comes from the observing assessor (the person who actually marked the in-tray, or observed the candidate in the group discussion) than when it is the result of their individual or collective evaluation of the evidence. Consensus may therefore be attained through the avoidance of discussion rather than through genuine, objective agreement. Furthermore, assessors will pay more attention to the evidence presented when they have to listen to the evidence being read out, and then provide their own independent rating, as opposed to simply concurring with the announced rating. Quite frankly, and we are not telling tales, the wash-up can become boring, and assessors can 'switch off' if the procedures do not require their active concentration and involvement. We have heard assessors read out the wrong set of evidence, and their colleagues happily provide a rating for it under the wrong heading.

In practice, assessors may choose to discuss the evidence by competency or by exercise. That means considering each cell relating to competency 1, and then competency 2, and so on; or each cell relating to the in-tray exercise, then the group discussion, etc. The survey of assessment centre practice found no pattern to the way assessors report their observations. In the context of competency-based selection, we would argue that the former approach – by competency – should always be preferred.

Combine the evidence for each competency into an overall competency rating

Once the individual scores or ratings are agreed, they can be assembled into a competency by exercise matrix for each candidate, just like Table 9.1. Faced with these ratings, the next task for assessors is to decide on an overall competency rating, for each of the competencies. Again there are

---

[1]   Reproduced by kind permission of Blackwells Publishers

two typical ways to do this – discussion (human judgement), or averaging (equations). In practice, the procedure seems to be a mixture of both. Typically, assessors will talk over results first to get an agreed score or rating (as discussed in the previous section), and then apply an equation to these agreed ratings, usually averaging, to produce an overall competency rating. Seventy-six per cent of respondents to the survey reported doing it this way, 20 per cent used a strict averaging method, i.e. took asessors' ratings at face value, and 4 per cent did it some other way.

The exercise effect revisited

If you have read Chapter 9, you may at this point be wondering how assessors deal with the exercise effect. In practice, assessors seem to find little difficulty in accepting that a candidate's influencing skills in a one-to-one role play may well be quite different to her influencing skills in a group discussion. Different contexts elicit different aspects of the competency, but to the assessors they are recognizably and conceptually part of the same competency. The wash-up process seeks to establish the candidate's scope for generalizing behaviour associated with the competency or their flexibility in applying the competency across varied situations.

Not all evidence is equally strong

There is one important qualifier which has to be taken into the reckoning when looking to combine evidence about a person's competence at an assessment centre. Exercises vary in the extent to which they elicit good evidence, and therefore in the extent to which ratings can be relied on. In general, the more the exercise demands actual work-related behaviour, and the more *direct* the observation, the stronger the evidence will be. Figure 10.1 shows what can be expected from various assessment centre methods. Thus, in the wash-up, you would generally give more weight to a role-play exercise, which provides evidence that is directly observed *and* work-related, than to a personality questionnaire, which provides second-hand (self-report) evidence, and is not directly work-related. Interviews fall in between because although work-related they are self-report.

It follows, then, that straightforward, unweighted averaging is unlikely to do justice to the data, so there has to be some form of weighting. This can be done by the assessors during their discussion. For example, a nine (top rating) on a personality questionnaire should not be allowed to drive up an overall rating when there are fives or even ones on direct measures. Although seldom done, this procedure can also be formalized into a

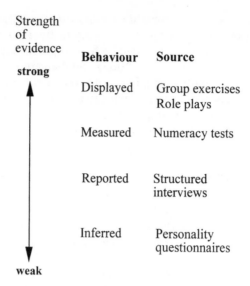

Figure 10.1   How Assessment Centre Exercises Compare on Strength of Evidence

weighted equation, with the direct measures attracting the greatest weights. As it is, assessors tend to operate a kind of informal weighting.

Make the decision, either through combination or separation

We began this section by outlining two possible approaches to making the final decision – combination of overall competency ratings, or separation.

Combination

Overall competency ratings can be combined simply, by adding them up or averaging them, or in a more complex way using weighted equations. In the UK at least, this is more common than may be supposed. The assessment centre survey found that 54 per cent of organizations produced some form of overall assessment rating (or 'OAR'). While in some cases OARs were produced on the basis of overall competency ratings, in others this stage was missed out altogether and the OAR was arrived at by using ratings from individual cells.

We have already noted that decisions made using statistical aggregation of data can be expected to be as good if not better than human decisions. To back this up, no single study has shown consensus-based overall assessment ratings (OARs) to be more predictive than mechanically derived OARs[5]. One study correlated a consensus-derived OAR and a mechanical OAR with five criteria. The mechanical OAR correlated significantly with all of the criteria whereas the consensus OAR correlated significantly with only one criterion.[6]

Mechanically derived OARs are also cheaper. Another study[7] estimated that the total cost of the wash-up session was 25–30% of the total AC cost, implying that using an equation to make decisions is quicker and therefore cheaper.

Separation

There is no doubt that keeping ratings separate, particularly overall competency ratings, allows for more sophisticated decision making. This will also be beneficial in the context of a competency-based human resource system, as detailed feedback on development needs can be taken forward for successful candidates. If it can be agreed, either through the results of job analysis or by expert judgement, which are the key competencies, then a series of *hurdles* can be defined, such as:

> On the nine-point scale, successful candidates must score:
> Seven or more on Achievement, Influencing and Problem solving
> No less than three on any competency.

Should this rule produce too many candidates, then the criteria can be made more stringent and re-applied to all candidates, for example:

> Seven or more on Achievement, Influencing and Problem Solving, no less than four on any competency.

This is precisely how the *immediate discard* method for sifting application forms works (Chapter 5). Importantly, the converse is not true. If there is no candidate who can clear the hurdles, then it becomes necessary to go out and recruit again. Certainly, there will be a temptation to lower the standard, and revisit some candidates ('he wasn't really so far off on that exercise'). Resist the temptation. A golden rule is never, ever to offer the job to the best of the rest. 'The best is the enemy of the good' is one of the truest adages we know.

If several candidates meet the standard, and there is more than one job, then individual competency profiles can be used to assist placement. If candidate X is strong on 'problem solving', and candidate Y is weaker but better at 'interpersonal skills', they might complement each other, or may fit into different areas of the organization more comfortably. In practice, assessment centre directors often employ hurdles without calling them such when they insist that no one with, say, a 'two' on any exercise, or on any competency, will be allowed through.

Hurdles in other contexts

Hurdles need not be reserved for assessment centres. The Inns of Court School of Law operated a hurdle procedure in the first year of selection. It worked as follows. There were four predictors which produced evidence for each candidate. A series of sweeps was made through the data with the hurdles (pass marks) on each of the four predictors being lowered at each sweep until a sufficient number of candidates had been selected to meet the entry target. The fact that some predictors were stronger than others (more valid and reliable) was allowed for by setting lower hurdles – relatively – on the weaker elements. For example, the hurdle for the supplementary application form – a kind of self assessment questionnaire – was always set much lower than ability test score (although that in itself stored up problems, as we have seen).

This is an example of what is known as a *conjunctive scoring model*[8]. The key point is that all hurdles must be successfully negotiated. Failure on one element cannot be compensated for by excellent performance on another. This is as it should be, for if we are measuring important criteria (competencies or whatever), candidates should be able to demonstrate some degree of competency on all of them – if not equally at least to a minimum standard. The use of *disjunctive* models, whereby exceeding the threshold is required in only one or perhaps two selection methods, and compensation is allowed in the rest, is quite common in the world of education. In the occupational sector, however, fully compensatory models are not so common. Indeed it is far more likely that candidates for jobs will be eliminated through a series of screens; in other words, a *progressive disjunctive* model will apply.

CONCLUSION

We have in effect presented practitioners with a dilemma. In essence, there are two approaches to decision making – asking people to make a judgement on the basis of ratings, or feeding the ratings into an equation (which as we have seen can take many forms). For recruitment and selection, we recommend that if the assessors are properly trained, and can be trusted, then the statistical method should be relied upon; their initial ratings should be aggregated and discretionary judgement, which is always lurking in the wings, ignored. There will always be some discussion, but this can be targeted. For example, the extremely good and extremely poor candidates will not require too much debate; it is usually the ones in the middle which will provoke arguments between assessors. There will also need to be some discussion of strengths and development needs for feedback purposes.

Trusting the assessors' ratings is an aspect of getting it right first time. You do not want an assessment process where too much energy goes into getting it right at the back end, and not enough into getting it right at the front end. Once you decide to have wash-ups, talk tends to expand to fill the time. Maybe, we need to review the need for them at all in the context of recruitment and selection, at least the ones that go into the night.

In summary, we would offer the following:

- try trusting the assessors and go with the numbers, without extended discussion

- if you cannot bring yourself to do this, hear the assessors' evidence first before asking for ratings, and then agree a rating

- allow for the varying strength of the methods by using weighted combination formulas to arrive at overall competency ratings, preferably explicitly

- if some competencies are definitely more important than others, set hurdles for those competencies and then evaluate candidates against these

- only select candidates who meet the standard, however defined

- if the preferred candidate turns you down, don't go for the next best unless they too have met the minimum criteria.

FEEDBACK

However the decision is taken, once it is taken candidates must be told about it. If you have stated your intention to give feedback to candidates, then Box 10.2 includes some points to bear in mind. They are offered in the spirit of countering what we called *casual implementation*.

BOX 10.2   GIVING FEEDBACK

- Feedback should only be given by those who are trained in and familiar with the instruments used.
- Feedback can be given face-to-face but this is not always possible with external candidates. In such cases it can be given by telephone or letter, with the opportunity to telephone the tester to discuss.
- Ask candidates first how they felt they did, before commencing feedback.
- Say what they did well, then what they did not do so well. Try to end on a high point.
- Be prepared to cite actual things they said or did, and ask them to tell you their significance.
- Tell them what you were looking for, and why they did not meet the standard.
- Never divulge actual test scores, i.e. percentiles; instead offer a rough guide on how performance compares to the relevant comparison group.
- Do not be judgmental with personality data – a person's approach to work is either appropriate or less appropriate to a particular job, not good or bad in itself.
- Do not give the impression that the decision was made solely on test or personality data.
- For unsuccessful candidates, stress that being unsuccessful simply meant that they were not right for the position, and that they have valuable strengths in other areas.

EVALUATION

Before putting the recruitment and selection process into mothballs until the next time, it is advisable to evaluate the whole process without delay. This exercise is helped greatly if an ongoing record has been kept of what the various players – assessors, candidates, administrators, consultants – had to say about elements of the process.

Working on total quality principles you will hope to have got everything right first time. But there will still be areas where you can improve; there always are. Start at the beginning, with the competencies. Are they still relevant? They almost certainly are, but were the behavioural indicators everything they might have been? Task someone with looking at those. Then there is the advertising – right placement, wrong placement?

Look at the number of responses, and their quality. If an RJP strategy was mounted, did it have the desired effect? What about the application form? Did the wording bring forth concise, relevant answers or was there some looseness which encouraged rambling, off-the-point answers? Did the sifting go well? If not, why not? Was it something about the guidelines – maybe too vague?

Now to the psychometrics. Did the tests do their job in excluding those who wouldn't make it, or were they too easy? Was the content always appropriate? Can the answers designated correct all be defended? Did the personality questionnaire throw up enough information to be worthwhile using next time? Are there better bets on the market?

The interview – did the prompts work as intended? Were some competencies harder to get at than others? What further questions are needed?

Next, to the assessment centre. How did the assessors perform? Is more training needed for some? Should any be politely dropped? Was the in-tray tight enough or are more distractors needed? Did the topic for the group discussion surface the behaviours being looked for? If roles were assigned, did this work or did the group subvert the exercise by getting the roles out into the open? How did the wash-up go? Was all the discussion warranted, and appropriate?

Finally, what did candidates – unsuccessful and successful – think about your process? Did it demand too much of their time? Did they feel that the methods used were giving them the opportunity to show their true mettle? What image might they have gained of your organization? Would they apply again if given the chance?

These are just some of the questions a thorough evaluation needs to ask. Getting things right first time must remain the objective but to succeed it is necessary to do all the right things, and in the right sequence. Of course, statistical validation is extremely desirable as well, but this will need to wait until you have assessed enough candidates. Better to build in quality than cross your fingers that the statistics will turn out okay. Competency-based recruitment and selection processes are multi-stage affairs, and the whole process is only as strong as its weakest link. Every design stage must be attended to if validation is to be claimed.

MONITORING

Finally, and a fitting note to end on given that we have tried to stress the need for objectivity and fairness throughout the book, we must emphasize the importance of monitoring. Specifically, we mean monitoring the results of your recruitment and selection process for signs of adverse impact on various groups within the population. These groups will include those covered by the equal opportunities legislation, but you may want to monitor the success of other groups depending on circumstances (for example public school/Oxbridge versus others in graduate recruitment, young versus older applicants, etc.). It is advisable to monitor all of the elements of the process individually, as well as the overall process and decision.

SUMMARY

In this final chapter we contrasted the application of human judgement with statistical judgement. We used the results to caution against over-reliance on assessors' discretionary judgement in the assessment centre wash-up (when the assessment centre is for selection only). We discussed various ways of combining ratings and pointed out the need to take into account, explicitly if possible, the reality that some methods provide stronger evidence than others. After providing some advice on giving feedback, we discussed ways of evaluating the process as a whole, and concluded with a plea to all professionals to monitor outcomes.

FETTERCORN plc – A CASE STUDY

'OK, so it's down to three,' said Jack. 'We've got Sally, Jim and Dee.'

'Hang on, hang on, we've got a process here,' Ros interjected. 'I know you all like Sally – she has great experience and is very personable, but she hasn't hit the criteria. We said at least a seven on 'Achievement Drive', and she only has a five. I'm sorry, but she has to go.'

'Good point,' said Jack. It was not a popular decision but to their credit, the assessors let the results speak for themselves.

'Right, so that's two left then. Let's just remind ourselves of the criteria – Jack, can you put them up on the OHP?' Jack obliged.

FETTERCORN CRITERIA

7 or more:
- Achievement drive
- Influencing
- Problem solving.

Minimum of two 5s and one 4:
- Learning ability
- Interpersonal skills
- Planning and organizing.

'Uh-oh . . . they've both passed, and we've only got one job.'

Jack said, 'Let's go over both candidates again. Put up Jim's scores.'

Jim

Achievement	8	Learning ability	6
Influencing	7	Interpersonal skills	4
Analytical thinking	7	Planning & organizing	8

'So, what's this saying to us?' asked Razia, one of the assessors. 'I think it's saying that Jim is pretty task-focused. His two highest scores are 'Achievement' and 'Planning' – this guy is sharp, focused and driven – he will get things done. The only worry is his interpersonal skills. He's going to have to get on with some pretty demanding senior managers inside the company, as well as building up rapport and relations with old and new suppliers. The question is – will he leave too many dead bodies on the way to the deal?'

'Nice summary. Ros, do you want to see Dee's scores?'

Dee

Achievement	8	Learning ability	6
Influencing	9	Interpersonal skills	8
Analytical thinking	6	Planning & organizing	5

'Right, Dee's also pretty driven . . . not so hot on the planning side. She may need some people around her who can make sure the detail gets done.'

'That ties in with her personality questionnaire profile – she's high on drive, and high on conceptual thinking, so she is likely to be drawn towards the bigger picture. In the feedback, she said she has moved on from dealing with the detail – other people do that for her now.'

'Thanks, Ros. Other high points are her interpersonal skills; she's likely to get on with other people, and use these skills to really get what she wants. Best of all, her influencing skills are superb. Everything else is fine.'

'So,' said Ros, 'the choice seems to come down to what we can live without: interpersonal skills, or planning and organizing skills.'

'Well in my experience, you can compensate for a lack of detail – you just provide good administrative support and an appropriate assistant. Interpersonal skills are hard to learn at this stage – my vote is for Dee,' said Sam.

Ros looked around the room. The other assessors nodded. She took a deep breath. 'Well, I think we have a decision then.'

'You must feel you got the right person,' said Jack to Ros. 'Dee had the best scores on the competencies which really counted.' 'Absolutely,' said Ros. 'Jim was close, but Dee definitely had the edge on 'influencing'. Her negotiating style looks very sharp. Some of our suppliers won't know what's hit them. And she's okay about the package because it was discussed in the interview. I know she wants to join us.'

As they sat reflecting on the day's events, an assessor came over. This was Edward Russell a.k.a. Eddie the Eagle or just Eagle, on account of his passion for skiing, and, what shall we say, his unusual technique. He had been very sceptical before the assessment centre, a right little prophet of doom. So much so that Ros had thought of dropping him. Now when she heard what he had to say she was very glad she hadn't. 'I know I said it wouldn't work, that it was a steam hammer to crack a nut. But it does work, it does. Especially seeing all the evidence.' 'Coming from you, Eagle, that's some praise.' Ros savoured the moment. There was no stopping the Eagle now. 'On the two exercises I observed him, I was sure Jim would be the one but now I see all the scores he isn't there, is he? If we'd just been interviewing, like we normally do, then he would have got it. I can't see us going back to interviews.' Let's press home the advantage, thought Ros. 'So how do you think you would have got on, Ed?' 'I'd have been brilliant, of course, especially on the group exercise, but I'd like to see some of the other buyers put through it, or something like it.' 'That can be arranged,' said Ros. Jack made a mental note to talk to Ros about development centres.

As Ed wandered off, Ros and Jack looked at each other with eyes open wide. High fives would have been in order, but they were British, and besides Lupita had just entered the room. 'Hi, Lupita,' Ros waved. 'I think we've got a Wayne Gretzky for the team.' Lupita frowned, 'Wayne Gretzky, who's he?' 'You know,' said Ros, 'hockey; we were talking about ice-hockey.' 'Oh, yes, hockey,' thinking Ros was mad. 'You must introduce me to Wayne.' 'It's Dee, actually, and she's going to be great.'

'Jack, we need to find time to talk this whole thing over.' Ros was back to her business-like self, no more messing around. Jack remembered someone calling her 'The Queen of Mean'. 'I'm happy about the competencies but I would like to revisit the interview prompts; I also think the in-tray needs tightening up, and one of the answers to one of the work sample tests doesn't look right. I'd also like your views on one or two of the assessors. Eddie was actually fine but Des seemed to lose the plot; it was obvious Razia had not kept any interview notes.' Jack nodded and took a quick peek at his diary. 'I can make it next Thursday. I'll bring along a little process we have for reviewing assessment centres. Now let me buy you that drink.' It was 7.15 and the Pig and Dongle beckoned.

REFERENCES

1. Wood, R., Hamer, G., Johnson, C.E. and Payne, T. (1997). Selecting for a profession: A case study. In Anderson, N.R. and Herriot, P. (Eds) *International Handbook of Selection and Assessment*. Chichester: Wiley.
2. Dawes, R.M., Faust, D. and Meehl, P.E. (1989). Clinical versus actuarial judgement. *Science*, **243**, 1668–74.
3. Pearn, M., Mulrooney, C. and Payne, T. (1998) *Learning from Mistakes: From Blame to Gain*. Aldershot: Gower.
4. Boyle, S., Fullerton, J. and Wood, R. (1995). Do assessment centres use optimum evaluation procedures? A survey of practice in UK organisations. *International Journal of Selection and Assessment*, **3**, 132–140.
5. Feltham, R. (1992). Assessment centre decision making: judgemental vs mechanical. *Journal of Occupational Psychology*, **61**, 237–241.
6. See reference 5.
7. Pynes, J. and Bernardin, H.J. (1992). Mechanical vs consensus-derived assessment center ratings: A comparison of job performance validities. *Public Personnel Management*, **21**, 17–28.
8. Green, B.F. and Wigdor, A.K. (Eds) (1988). *Measuring Job Competency*. Washington, DC: National Academy Press.

Index